IMPORTANT I

Do not use this book until you have read these pages.

You have in your hands one half of the system that will change your life. To achieve success it is essential that you download the other half of this system from the Hay House website:

hayhouse.com/mckenna

and use the audio session that completes it.

This is not just a book to read, it is part of a life-changing solution. This book is the first essential element of the system. The audio session is just as important: you must use both the book and the audio session to achieve permanent success.

The session contains everything I would do if I were working with you personally. It includes simple, powerful psychological techniques and a hypnotic trance that strengthen the power of your subconscious mind to guide your success.

The session is really easy to download onto your computer or smartphone, just a few clicks, then a few minutes later, you will have me there whenever you need, to help you make the changes you want.

Intellectual knowledge is not the same as real change, so you cannot expect lasting results if you only read this book. You must download and use the psychological techniques and guided hypnosis to achieve permanent, positive change.

In hypnotic trance your unconscious is highly receptive to positive intentions. It is not the same as sleep, it is a wonderful state of deep relaxation, like a daydream or meditation, and even though you are deeply relaxed, if for any reason you need to awaken, you will do so with all the resources you need.

The audio techniques are not just essential, they are also enjoyable and rewarding. In fact, many people use them over and over to reinforce their new mind-set and enhance their success.

Ensure your success now. Go online now to:

hayhouse.com/mckenna

1. Input the product ID and download code shown below (also found on the card at the front of this book) and then download the free session right now:

Product ID: 2316

Download code: mckenna

2. Regularly use the session as directed in this book.
3. Enjoy it and relax, knowing you are now on your way to lasting success!

I CAN MAKE YOU HAPPY

PAUL MCKENNA, PH.D.

EDITED BY HUGH WILLBOURN, PH.D.

HAY HOUSE, INC.
Carlsbad, California • New York City
London • Sydney • Johannesburg
Vancouver • New Delhi

Published and distributed in the United States by: Hay House, Inc.:
www.hayhouse.com® • *Published and distributed in Australia by:*
Hay House Australia Pty. Ltd.: www.hayhouse.com.au • *Published and
distributed in the United Kingdom by:* Hay House UK, Ltd.: www.hay-
house.co.uk • *Published and distributed in the Republic of South Africa by:* Hay House SA (Pty), Ltd.: www.hayhouse.co.za • *Distributed in
Canada by:* Raincoast Books: www.raincoast.com • *Published in India
by:* Hay House Publishers India: www.hayhouse.co.in

Cover design: Alex Tuppen

Previously published in Great Britain by Bantam Press, a division of
Transworld Publishers, ISBN: 9780593064047.

Cataloging-in-Publication Data is on file at the Library of Congress

Tradepaper ISBN: 978-1-4019-4901-3

10 9 8 7 6 5 4 3 2 1
1st Hay House edition, September 2016

Printed in the United States of America

I CAN MAKE YOU HAPPY

WARNING

DO NOT LISTEN TO THE AUDIO DOWNLOAD
WHILE DRIVING OR OPERATING HEAVY MACHINERY,
OR IF YOU SUFFER FROM EPILEPSY.
IF IN DOUBT, CONSULT YOUR DOCTOR.

IMPORTANT:
ABOUT THE HYPNOTIC
TRANCE DOWNLOAD

Accompanying this book you will find a powerful hypnotic trance download that will program your mind to build and enrich your happiness throughout your life. You can find the details on the special card at the front of the book.

It is best to listen to the trance when you have about half an hour to relax completely.

Do not use the hypnotic trance while driving or operating machinery.

Even if you didn't read a single word in this book and only used the hypnotic trance, you would still notice an amazing increase of happiness in your life.

Your mind is like a computer. It has its own software that organizes your thinking and behavior. Having worked with all sorts of people with different problems over the years, I have learned that almost all their problems were caused by a negative program running in the unconscious mind. This hypnotic trance helps you remove negative thinking and installs positive programs that seek out and magnify the factors that create your happiness. It guides the unconscious mind to assist you and boost the effect of all the exercises in the book.

The hypnotic trance also contains an amazing new process that delivers the same states of mind as 20 years of practice of meditation. You don't have to know anything about meditation and you don't have to believe in it. Just use the hypnotic trance and you can get the benefits of the technique.

The hypnotic element has been carefully crafted to work with you at the pace set by your own unconscious mind. It will help you to relax to the right level for you each time you use it. The benefits will become stronger and stronger each time you listen.

• • •

CHAPTER 1

•

Introduction

Introduction

You are about to have a life-changing experience. It doesn't matter whether you are sad, bored, down, depressed, doing all right, or quite happy—the system in this book will help you become a whole lot happier very soon.

The scientific research shows that happiness levels are not fixed. To increase your happiness levels takes a small amount of regular effort over a few days. Following simple instructions and using some powerful psychological techniques, you can transform your life. You will create a strong underlying feeling of happiness every day and have more and more times of realizing rich, deep, fulfilling happiness throughout your life.

This is a factual, practical book. I suggest you test everything to see how it works. Please don't just take it on trust. Make sure that everything you do works for you.

My techniques draw on the most recent scientific and psychological advances and I have tested every technique in this system personally over and over again. In the last 25 years I have worked with people who are totally and utterly depressed and people who are happy, and I have figured out the difference between the two. Surprisingly it comes down to just a few small but important differences in the way they think and act. Those differences have a massive effect on the quality of your life.

To make yourself happier, all you have to do is to follow some simple instructions every day.

Cut Out the Middleman

In the West lots of people spend time and effort getting things they believe will make them happy, like new clothes or a new car. Sometimes it works for a while, but the good feeling fades quickly and they need another new thing to make them happy. So they spend more time and effort and money to buy the next thing.

The system in this book and hypnotic trance takes a different route. This book increases your happiness directly. Think of all the things you'd like to have right now. Take a moment to list the top ten things you really want. Now think of them all and ask yourself, when I have these, how will I feel? When you get them, you will feel good. Ultimately, when you buy anything you are buying good feelings. As you use the system in this book, you can cut out all those middlemen and increase your happiness right now.

There are lots of different techniques in the book and, depending on your psychology, some will work more quickly than others. So, even if at first you feel just one or two have an immediate impact, surely it is worth reading the whole book and using all the exercises to find which ones work best in the long term.

Happiness Is Natural

Happiness is a natural human state, like hunger, anger, excitement, boredom, neutrality, and alertness. Absolutely everyone can be happy. Happiness is how the mind and body guide you towards what is most rewarding for you. Happiness is not just a pleasurable sensation. When you are on a path that brings you happiness, it will guide you, perhaps in surprising ways, to more happiness.

We are all born with the ability to be happy, and however happy or unhappy you are now, you can be happier. I've worked with people who thought they were happy enough but were amazed to discover there is no upper limit to happiness.

I've worked with people who had everything—a great job, a family, and good health—but they were still not happy. They felt guilty and angry with themselves for not enjoying their good fortune. They said they were so depressed they couldn't see any point in their lives. I took them through this system and they began changing. They didn't believe it would work at first, and when they started to feel happier they weren't sure it would last, but their lives did change, and when you look back in a few weeks, your life will be different.

I've seen people who believed they had never really been happy, and people who had been given every negative label under the sun. Some people came to see me when they were exhausted by the emotional roller coaster of their life. They achieved a real shift and started to experience a richer and brighter life.

I've seen scientists amazed at how people who were supposedly permanently depressed shifted the neurological activity in their brain by repeatedly using the simple psychological techniques in this book. They became happier than they ever thought possible. In just a short time they noticed the changes in their feelings and they began to see themselves differently.

It is wonderful to see people who have been depressed for 25 years find the heavy black cloud of depression starting to disappear and begin to experience lightness entering their life.

Fear of Happiness

It might seem strange, but a few of the people with whom I have worked were actually frightened of being happy. They worried that they would feel good, but that after a time the feeling would fade and they would feel worse than before because they would know too much about what they were missing. So every time they get happy, they stop. That is like driving down the road with your foot on the accelerator and then slamming on the brakes. You don't have to do that. If you have been let down in the past, use this system very slowly. Do one exercise at a time and take as long as you need to get used to it before moving on. That way you will be sure that you know how to feel happy and keep that happiness before you move to the next stage.

Other people were frightened that if they felt happy they would relax too much. If they were not dissatisfied, they would not be hungry for achievement so they'd lose their edge. If they saw the whole world through rose-colored glasses, they wouldn't be able to reason or judge things rationally. But even the frightened ones found they could be happier, and they didn't lose their drive.

As they used this system, each person experienced more and more moments and waves of happiness. Some were skeptical. Although they were changing a bit more each day, they didn't even know it was happening until they noticed how far they had come.

Everyone has slightly different experiences, but as you have more and more happy times, you begin to build a richer, deeper feeling of lasting happiness and contentment that becomes the background of your life.

I Can Make You Happy

Just in case you think this is all too good to be true, let's also get clear what this means. Increasing your happiness does not mean we can get rid of all the pain, difficulty, irritation, and suffering in your life. It does not mean I can make you permanently ecstatic all day long every day. Also, it doesn't mean being up all the time.

It does mean that happiness will play a larger part in your life. You will notice being happy more often. You will find that you don't need particular things or events to trigger happiness—it just comes over you. You will notice that the background mood of your life is happier. You will experience more frequent episodes of joy and happiness, love and gratitude. But it also means having and appreciating a full dynamic range of emotions. As we shall see later, all your emotions, even the uncomfortable ones, are valuable. This range means that you don't just enjoy life, you build a sense of fulfillment.

If you have been feeling depressed or seriously down or bored or sad, you will find that this system begins to change your life, and one day you will notice that you have begun to think of yourself as a happy person. Even when bad things happen—and they do happen to all of us—you will feel resilient and confident. Because you are a happy person, you will be able to meet whatever challenges come your way and return to your natural state of happiness.

Being happy helps you to make changes in your life that bring even more happiness into your life. The happier you are, the more reasons you will create to be happier still.

We Are Going to Program Your Mind to Be Happier

From time to time, people tell me they believe something inside them is broken. However you might feel, you are not broken. You have simply picked up some unhelpful ways of thinking and acting that are making you feel bad. They have been reinforced and this affects your brain chemistry, which in turn continues the pattern. The system in this book will help you to interrupt that pattern and change it. You will replace the unhelpful ways of thinking with habits that create happiness. By practicing the techniques and using the hypnotic trance every day, you will reinforce a new set of thoughts and feelings so it will become natural to feel better and better.

Failure

Occasionally somebody says to me, "I read your book and it didn't work." Immediately, I pay attention. I've spent years and years developing, testing, and using these techniques and working out how to transmit them clearly and safely, so I always ask exactly what they did and how it didn't work. Every time, I discover the same thing: They haven't actually followed the instructions. They haven't finished reading the book, or they didn't use the techniques, or they didn't listen to the hypnotic trance. They used the techniques just once. They only practiced three of them. They listened to half the hypnotic trance and they were interrupted. Or they read the book and thought, "Yeah, I understand all that," and assumed they didn't need to actually practice the techniques. But understanding is not the same as practice. If I want to learn to tie my shoelaces, I just have to practice. You have to practice so often that you can do what you need to do without thinking about it.

How It Works

It may be that you are so close to increasing your happiness that all it takes is reading one particular chapter or doing just one exercise to make you feel great.

But of course I don't know the exact circumstances in which you are reading this book. I don't know the specific details of how you have built up your understanding of your situation. And I don't want you to have just a boost of happiness for a day or two or a week and then go back to where you were.

I want to make sure that you make a genuine shift to a position where you can enjoy more happiness in your life and you have the ability to increase and sustain that happiness whatever happens around you. When you understand that you have the power to determine your response to what happens, you create a genuine, strong foundation of happiness that allows you to make it through hard times and fully enjoy every opportunity for joy. So even though you may start to achieve success early on in the book, it's important to read through the whole book, step by step, and use all the techniques and the hypnotic trance to make sure you build the foundations correctly to achieve and sustain a lasting increase in happiness.

Techniques

Each technique is a practical step on the path to building deep, robust happiness. It is essential that you follow the instructions completely. Don't worry if it takes you a few times to get it just right. Keep practicing and repeat them over and over again. These techniques will become a natural part of your life so you can do them whenever you need them without any hesitation.

Now, it is true that not everyone has to do all of these exercises all the time in order to be happy. Most of us find that two or three of them make the difference we need and set the ball rolling to increase our happiness. But as I have not met you personally, I cannot predict which specific techniques are going to work best for you. So to guarantee good results you need to do all of them. Then it is likely that you will have one or two favorites and it is absolutely fine to use those as much as you wish.

In this system I have included some techniques that I have used in other books because they simply are the most powerful and efficient ways to get the results you need.

The Hypnotic Trance Download

Accompanying this book is a hypnotic trance to make you happier. The suggestions within the trance bypass the filters of the conscious mind, so regardless of what you think and whatever is happening at a conscious level, the positive messages are absorbed at the deeper levels of your mind. You don't have to try to listen to my words, you can relax as much as you want and it will work for you. As you relax, I will communicate directly with your unconscious mind and give you hypnotic suggestions that work alongside all the techniques and instructions in the book. They install and reinforce ways of thinking about the world that make you happier. The suggestions are crafted to enhance your inner resources and empower you to pursue your own unique route to fulfillment and happiness. The trance and the suggestions become more powerful each time you use them, so it is important to use the hypnotic trance repeatedly.

Within the trance I will also introduce you to the process discovered by my friend Genpo Roshi, which allows people with no prior knowledge of meditation to experience the state of blissful calm that mystics have sought for centuries.

Genpo Roshi is a Zen Master who has combined elements of Zen meditation and Western psychology to allow us to move straight to the core experiences of meditation. I consider this to be the most advanced form of meditation to have been developed since Buddhism came to the West.

His procedure, called Big Mind, permits the limitations of everyday consciousness to stand aside so that the primordial bliss of awareness is manifest and you can relax into it completely. This deep sense of bliss is profoundly healing and nourishing. It will refresh you, restore your energy, and install a deep sense of love and optimism. Within the frame of the trance your mind will experience this process as gently and as deeply as is best for you each time you listen.

Use this hypnotic trance at least once every day for the next two weeks. You can listen to it more often than that and for as long as you want. When you want to listen to it, find a comfortable place where you can relax deeply without distraction. Do not listen to the hypnotic trance while driving or operating machinery.

How Do I Know How to Make You Happy?

I'm not a guru. I don't have all the answers. But I've been working and researching with people for decades. I don't have magic powers but I do have a skill set. I have developed it over years of relentless pursuit of the quickest, most reliable ways to create permanent positive psychological change. I have refined these methods so that when you use them you will absolutely increase the happiness in your life.

Although I didn't realize it, I have been collecting the material for this book for years. I have worked with hundreds of thousands of people to help them change their lives for the better. I've learned a great deal from the people with whom I have worked and from people who are already happy. I've spent time observing what they do and say, and how they perceive things. They're not scientists or gurus or mystics or intellectuals, they are just happy people.

And my own path through life so far has taught me a thing or two. I've had ups and downs, successes and failures. And I've learned that all our actions have a positive and negative potential, and every "failure" can become a lesson and every "success" opens the door to a new challenge. And I am still learning.

Throughout this book I will share with you stories from my life, from my colleagues, and from my clients. Some are rich and famous and some are not, but I have found that money and fame ultimately make no difference. In terms of learning to be more happy, we are all equal.

How Do You Feel Right Now?

Before we go any further, please answer the following question:

On a scale of 1 to 10, where 1 is as low as possible and 10 is as high as possible, how happy do you feel about your life overall?

If you score between 1 and 3, go straight to Chapter 2, which is the section with a gray edge on the pages. Chapter 2 is crafted to pick you up right now so that you are fully prepared to benefit from the rest of the system.

If you score between 4 and 10 you can go straight to Chapter 3.

You should also read Chapter 2 if you agree with any or all of the statements on the next page . . .

"I feel so low, I don't really
think anything can help"

"I feel really depressed,
but I don't know why"

"Right now, happiness feels
a million miles away"

"I used to think I was
happy, but it was just
an illusion"

"I've never really
been happy, I just
thought I was"

"I want to be happy,
but I feel that it is
not my destiny"

"I don't deserve
to be happy"

"I used to be so
happy, but I never
will again"

"I don't know how
to be happy"

"I can't be happy—
there is just too much
stacked up against me"

"This book won't
work either"

"It's a nice idea, but it
won't work for me"

"I'm worried this book
will make me worse"

"I'm so messed up I don't
know where to start"

And any other time you feel low, or you need a rapid boost to get you going again, turn to Chapter 2 and use the techniques to lift you up.

CHAPTER 2

•

The Instant
Pick-Me-Up

The Instant Pick-Me-Up

I know what it's like to feel totally and utterly depressed, to see no point in anything, to not care if I live or die, to be completely unable to find any value in anything. I have spent time feeling life was pointless and I have found my way back to everyday life and on to real, lasting, amazing happiness. On the way I created a map of how I found my way back, I have tested it on people who were in the darkest of places and it works. I have spent a lot of time in the minds of depressed people building a bridge out of the darkness and now I want to do it for you.

That's what this book is. It's not a bunch of theories, it's a practical system that will help you find your way to a richer, happier life today.

How to Get Out of a Dark Place Right Now

There are some simple things you need to do that will start to change how you feel now. The techniques in this chapter are easy to do, and anyone can do them. However, some people reading this may already feel worried that they won't be able to do them, they'll get it wrong, or the techniques won't work. All these thoughts are natural, automatic consequences of feeling very low, because it is a symptom of feeling low to underestimate our abilities.

So, first of all, if you feel a bit unsure, only do as much as is comfortable. Read one paragraph at a time and do the first exercise at a pace that feels comfortable. Don't rush it, just do it one step at a time. With all of these exercises it doesn't matter if you take it in really, really small steps. If you take one tiny step, take a rest and then take another, then little by little you will get moving in the right direction.

Secondly, don't put pressure on yourself by expecting to understand everything right now. Just follow the instructions one step at a time.

Brain Chemistry

Feeling depressed is a physical state. It is not just "all in the mind." Over the last ten years, Dr. Candace Pert has done some pioneering work that demonstrates clearly that our moods and understanding are not just electrical impulses in the brain. They are also coded in the neuropeptides or "messenger molecules" that are released into our bloodstream. Scientists have known for a long time about the effects of adrenaline and the endorphins. Now, it seems, they are discovering that there are many, many other neuropeptides correlated to our moods. So when you are very down, there are chemicals in your body that correspond to that low feeling. By the same token, feeling good corresponds to different neuropeptides. Your body produces chemicals that make you happy and change your body at the cellular level.

One reason that people get down is that the levels of serotonin and other happiness neurotransmitters in their brain have fallen too low. Many of us know what it is like to wake at 3 A.M. and find ourselves thinking that life is terrible. This happens because, in order to let us dream, our bodies stop producing norepinephrine and serotonin, so we don't have our normal buffers and defensive system. When we wake in the morning everything looks much better just because we have our normal complement of neurotransmitters available to help us deal with things.

A similar problem can occur if our happiness brain chemistry is depleted during the day. This can be caused by overwork, by excessive drug use, or even a poor diet. It is therefore worth going to see your doctor for a checkup. Even a simple thing like changing your diet can make all the difference.

The techniques in this chapter will all make a physical change in your brain chemistry. You already have the capacity to make "happy chemicals" inside you, but it hasn't been working very hard, and it hasn't produced enough of them. We are going to get your body making more of those happy chemicals right now!

Feeling Good

There is a lot more to happiness than feeling good, but it is a good place to start. More importantly, when you feel better, it is easier to make the bigger changes that install real happiness in your life.

The five exercises in this chapter will all change your immediate physical state. You will feel better. There may still be things in your life that you are unhappy about, and there may well be a lot more to do. You may even be thinking that changing how you feel really doesn't count for much given all the pain in your past and challenges you may face in the future. Actually, it will make a huge difference, because it gives you a safe, solid platform from which you can operate to make bigger changes. So whether you feel open-minded or thoroughly cynical, just use these techniques and follow the instructions. When you feel more comfortable you will be in a better position to make good choices about what to do next.

The Power of Posture

The mind and body are linked. Tense your body and your thoughts become tense. Relax your thoughts and your body relaxes.

From yoga and the ancient martial arts to modern disciplines such as Pilates and the Alexander Technique, human beings have used movement and posture to create a state of calm, balance, and well-being. All these techniques make use of the linkage between the mind and the body to change your psychological state. One of the most powerful, simple techniques to improve our mood is at the heart of all of these disciplines and yet it doesn't require any training at all.

Typically, when we are not particularly happy we tend to slouch a bit, let our heads hang down a little, and our shoulders come forward. This posture is universally associated with low spirits. In fact, if you felt fine and then spent half an hour slouching forward you would make your mood less comfortable. Don't do that! In fact, I'm suggesting you do the exact opposite.

When you get into that upright, relaxed, balanced posture, your body will make you feel better.

HAPPY POSTURE

Read the whole exercise through before you start.

- The easiest way to get into this posture, whether you are sitting or standing, is to imagine there is a silver thread coming down from the sky that is gently pulling you up from the very top of your head. Imagine letting that thread hold your head upright.

- Now let your shoulders drop down and back, feel your back being lifted up by your neck, and feel the gentle, upright, long, S-shaped curve of your back supporting you, and your head floating on your shoulders.

- Finally let your shoulders drop a bit more. Imagine that silver thread is holding your head up and let it support your whole body. With each breath, let yourself relax a bit more, keeping that upright stance, and stay like that for at least one minute.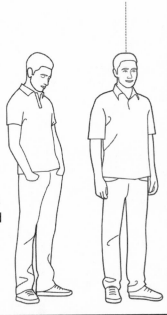

This is very, very simple and yet it is so good for you. It moves you away from a sad or depressed posture and begins to open you up to feeling happy.

Think about this and do it consciously for a few moments over and over again every day so that you build the habit of naturally sitting or standing in a comfortable, relaxed, upright position. Even a very small shift towards a more relaxed and upright posture can allow a really large increase in comfort and happiness to build up over a period of days and weeks. But, just like everything else in this book, don't just read it or think about it—do it and prove to yourself that it works.

How to Stop an Unhappy Feeling Quickly

Even after you have started this process of change, the chances are you will occasionally get surprised by unhappy feelings, just because you have accumulated habits associated with feeling unhappy. It is not deliberate, it is an accident. You notice something that triggered a feeling of sadness or feeling low in the past and it does so again, just because of the association. You have already started changing these associations, but you can't change everything all at once, so this technique gives you an alternative if you notice that, for whatever reason, you begin to feel down.

The technique involves changing your habitual line of sight. People who feel low tend to look downwards and they don't see much further than the ground a few yards in front of them. That causes a feeling of being hemmed in with few possibilities, and it is strongly associated with feeling bad. People who look up frequently stretch their gaze all the way to the sky or the horizon and that automatically suggests space and the freedom of lots of possibilities.

These differences have a strong influence on our thinking. However, there is much more to it than that. Scientists have shown that there is a hardwired connection between our eye movements and our patterns of thought and feelings. There is an observable change in brain activity when people look upwards that is associated with the visual cortex and tends to cause the brain to generate more alpha waves, which develops feelings of peace, comfort, and well-being. If we also move our eyes from side to side, it breaks down the associations that were making you unhappy.

Again, it seems almost ridiculous that something so simple can have such a powerful effect, but the science shows that it works. People sometimes are skeptical when I tell them how powerful it is. I always tell them, "The best way to find out that it works is to do it."

INSTANT RESCUE

Read the whole exercise through before you start and rehearse it so that you can go straight through the whole sequence without looking at the book.

Use this to change your immediate experience and you will be free to feel something much more comfortable.

1. Use this technique whenever you feel low. To practice it now, remember a time when you felt unhappy, just enough to have a bit of that feeling again.

2. Now look upwards at the ceiling for at least 30 seconds as if you were trying to see the tips of your eyebrows and you sense just a slight strain on your eye muscles.

3. Now, keeping your head still and keeping aware of that feeling, slowly move your eyes from side to side, so that you are looking up left and then up right, back and forth 20 times.

Continued

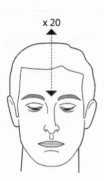

4. Now, with your head still, look up and down 20 times.

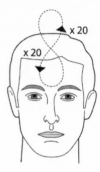

5. Now, still keeping aware of the feeling, even as it is diminishing, move your eyes in a figure eight 20 times, and then in a figure eight in the other direction 20 times.

6. Now look straight ahead and notice how much you have reduced the feeling. If you want to reduce it further repeat steps 2, 3, 4 and 5.

7. Do not let yourself look downwards for any length of time until you feel okay again.

8. If you feel any miserable feelings coming again, look up again and go back to step 2.

Any action you repeat often enough will strengthen the neural pathways that drive it, so as you do this more and more often, you build up new neural pathways and new associations that move you automatically away from miserable feelings towards good feelings. You rewire your brain so that the original pattern is interrupted and the trigger actually becomes associated with moving towards feeling better.

Happy Vision

As soon as you have mastered the Instant Rescue technique, you can boost its effect by developing a habit of looking upwards frequently each day. Look at the sky and admire the clouds. Look up at the tops of buildings and notice all the architectural features up there. It is quite interesting looking up, but much more important, it continually triggers your brain to reinforce good feelings.

Havening

Havening therapy was created by my friend Ronald Ruden, M.D., Ph.D. Scientific studies have shown that it is amazingly effective at relieving sadness and reducing stress, trauma, and compulsion. Dr. Ruden's work has been hailed as a remarkable breakthrough. He discovered that patterns of repeated touch to parts of the body combined with specific eye movements and visualizations have a rapid, reliable, and predictable effect on our feelings. His years of research have created a significant advance in what is known as "psychosensory therapy." The patterns of touch used in Havening are what enable a mother to comfort her baby and are hardwired into every infant. Havening combines these deep-rooted patterns of reassurance and comfort with sequences to break down the associations that triggered unhappy feelings. As a result, in just a few minutes we can now reduce the intensity of an emotion or feeling of unhappiness and establish calm, robust relaxation.

This technique is not merely a distraction. Studies have shown that when we use the Havening technique, we reduce stress chemicals in our body and produce states of relaxation and calm. We also change the way our brain processes thoughts and feelings. The effect of the specific sequence I will share with you is to reset the way your brain interprets and responds to stress. Over time this actually alters the neuronal pathways in your brain.

A SAFE HAVEN

Please read through the following exercise before you do it. You should practice this sequence of eye movements, body touches, and visualizations several times until you know it by heart. Then you will be able to use it any time you need to get rid of unhappy feelings and swiftly feel calm and relaxed.

1. Notice how much unhappiness or sadness you feel and rate it on a scale of 1 to 10. This is important, because it lets you measure how much you reduce it.

2. Now clear your mind, or just think about something nice.

Continued

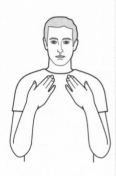

3. Next, use both hands to tap on both your collarbones.

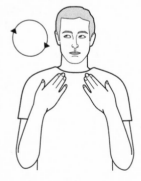

4. While you continue tapping on both your collarbones, look straight ahead, keep your head still, and close and open your eyes.

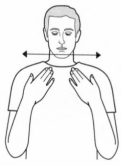

5. Continue tapping and, keeping your head still, look down to the left then down to the right.

6. Continue tapping, keeping your head still, and move your eyes in a full circle clockwise and then counterclockwise.

Continued

7. Now cross your arms, place your hands on top of your shoulders, and close your eyes.

8. Now stroke your hands down the sides of your arms from your shoulders to your elbows and up again, down and up, again and again.

1, 2, 3......19, 20

9.

9. As you carry on stroking the sides of your arms, imagine you are walking down a flight of stairs and count out loud from 1 to 20 with each step you take.

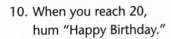

10. When you reach 20, hum "Happy Birthday."

Continued

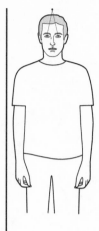

11. Now let your arms drop and relax them, and open your eyes and look up in front of and above you.

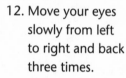

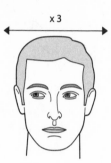

12. Move your eyes slowly from left to right and back three times.

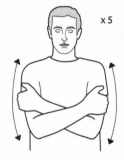

13. Close your eyes and stroke the sides of your arms again five times.

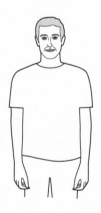

14. Now open your eyes and check, on your scale from 1 to 10, what number the feeling is at now.

If it is way down at the bottom, congratulations—you have personally changed your own feeling state. If you think the unhappy feeling is not yet reduced enough, just repeat the Havening sequence until it is reduced as far as you want.

Reality and Imagination

Scientists researching the workings of the brain have discovered that at a neurological level the brain reacts in the same way to vivid imagination as it does to reality. For example, you only have to imagine walking down a dark alley late at night and hearing footsteps behind you and your heartbeat will quicken. But if you vividly remember a time you felt wonderfully relaxed on vacation, your heartbeat will slow down and you'll begin to feel calmer.

As we saw earlier, we also know that our posture affects how we feel. We can use these two facts to kick-start your happiness project. You can vividly imagine someone who is happy and then take on their posture and that will create in you the happy feelings they experience.

Happy people have a lot of characteristics in common. They smile easily and find many opportunities to enjoy themselves even in everyday situations. They take time for both relaxation and activity and they have a sense of purpose in life. They are good-humored, they have good friends, and they are friendly to strangers without rushing to get too involved. They don't worry much and are grateful for their good fortune. They look relaxed, at ease, friendly, and welcoming.

THE HAPPY STEP-IN

Read the whole exercise through before you start.

1. Think of someone you know or admire who is very happy.

2. Vividly imagine them standing in front of you. Notice what they are wearing, how they are standing, where they are looking, and what they are doing.

3. Now imagine them turning around so you are behind them, and now imagine stepping into that person, so that you see through their eyes, and actually physically copy their posture now. Stand as they stand, breathe as they breathe, and experience their feelings.

4. Notice where the good feelings are strongest in your body and spread those feelings all around—up to the top of your head and down to the tip of your toes.

5. Now imagine taking this feeling into your everyday life.

Polarity Responders

Have you ever made a set of bad choices that caused you unhappiness and wondered why that happened? There are some people who have an automatic tendency to disagree with any suggestion, even if it is a positive one, before they have a chance to think about it.

I had a woman in a seminar once who was like that. On the second day I pointed out that she had reacted against everything that was offered on the first day and I suggested she was a polarity responder. Quick as a flash she came back with, "No, I'm not." We all laughed—and when she realized what she had said, so did she.

Disagreeing is actually a very basic form of defense. Polarity responders are people who in the past have been tricked or betrayed. If you notice that tendency yourself when you are reading this book, don't fight it. Let yourself voice that disagreement, but then look again at what is offered, and see if there is something useful in it for you. If you work through all of these techniques you will be happier and safer and free from being a polarity responder.

Making Space for Change

When you use the first four exercises, you create a basic positive feeling in the present that is your starting point for a deep and lasting increase in your personal happiness. Simply using and repeating these exercises will improve your mood, and that helps you take the next step towards changing your whole life for the better.

The final exercise in this chapter, which opens up the space to make bigger changes, is very, very simple and yet deceptively powerful. When you are not being pulled and pushed by your emotions, you create more freedom to choose where to direct your attention and what you wish to change. It's like getting a bit of shelter from the wind so that you can catch your breath and look around.

In order to create the space and connection to work with your emotions, the first step is to create stillness so that you can observe them. At this point, we don't need to do any more than that. We are just going to take a few minutes to create an inner stillness so that our emotions can come and go.

STILLNESS

Read the whole exercise through before you start.

1. Sit still somewhere you can be undisturbed for a while, with no music, TV, or radio. Sit upright with your hands in your lap and your feet flat on the floor.

2. Focus on your breathing—let it become easier and more regular.

3. Then focus on how you feel. The easiest place to start is to pay attention to the solar plexus area at the front of your body below your rib cage and above your navel.

4. In a calm, gentle voice, describe each of the feelings you experience in your body. For example, "I notice a fluttering in my stomach," "I have a soft, tired feeling in my arms," or "I feel the tension in my shoulders melting." You don't have to be perfectly accurate, just do the best you can. Don't try to change it yet, and don't get carried away. Keep moving your attention from your breathing to your solar plexus and then back to your breathing.

5. Do this for just two minutes and then take a break.

CHAPTER 3

•

The Habits
of Happiness

The Habits of Happiness

When you were a child you learned how to use a handle to open a door. Pretty soon you generalized that learning so that you knew how to open all doors. If we didn't do that, each day we would have to learn how to go in and out of a room all over again. Each learning becomes a habit that you store in your unconscious mind. Habits help us live our lives efficiently.

You create habits by repetition. Each one of our thoughts and actions corresponds to a neural pathway in the brain. The more we repeat a thought or action, the stronger that pathway becomes, just as a footpath across a field becomes more clear and firm the more people walk along it.

Habits are regulated directly by the unconscious mind. That's why I have included the hypnotic trance with this book. When you listen to it, I talk to your unconscious mind and the hypnotic suggestions help to reprogram those habits, just like downloading a software update to your computer.

We have habits in every part of our life—from gestures, to how we talk, what we eat, and where we like to go on vacation. We also have habits of thinking and feeling. Unhappy people have habits that maintain their state, and happy people have habits that sustain their happiness.

Changing Habits

A habit is like a river of energy. That energy never disappears. We need to use it, either by substituting a new habit or by redirecting it to a different outcome. We can do that by using the energy it contains and diverting its course. We need to catch it near the beginning and send it in a different direction. It is just like digging a little ditch to divert water from a stream. At first, only a small fraction of the water goes in the new direction, but as it does so it makes the new route a little deeper and wider, so more water flows that way. Little by little you change the course of the whole stream.

The exercises in this chapter will help you change your habits. Each time you practice an exercise you make the new behavior easier and more powerful.

Change Is Possible

My friend Dr. Robert Holden, who is often referred to as the "happiness psychologist," has conducted an amazing experiment to show that we can easily and completely alter levels of happiness just by changing our habits. Rather than trying to break habits, he replaced the old ones with new ones. He just added experiences to people's lives that make them feel good.

Robert's work was the subject of a BBC documentary. He took a group of depressed people through an extraordinary experiment that lasted for several weeks. At the beginning of the experiment all the subjects were all given an MRI scan. The scan focused on the activity in the left prefrontal lobe in an area that corresponds with happy thoughts and feelings and it showed they had the signs associated with depression.

Robert's remarkably simple formula to increase their happiness was to ask his depressed subjects to do three things:

- Smile or laugh for at least 20 minutes a day.
- Take at least 20 minutes' exercise every day.
- Place colored dots around every room of their home and at their work. Whenever they saw a colored dot they had to think about a positive memory, event, or possibility.

His subjects followed this regime for a month. At the end of that time, every single one of them reported that they felt happier. They were all then given another MRI scan and it showed they had significantly increased activity in the left prefrontal lobe area. In one month, Robert's subject had changed the physical activity of their neural networks and brain chemistry by changing their habits of thinking and behavior. They had moved from being depressed to extremely optimistic.

These findings were so remarkable that the independent psychologist the BBC had asked to monitor the experiment insisted that the MRI machine be checked for faults. The machine was working perfectly. But the BBC bosses were still wary, so they delayed transmitting the program for six months because they couldn't believe the change would last. Six months later the subjects took another MRI scan. The changes were still there and the subjects also reported that they still felt significantly happier.

Three Magical Habits of Happiness

Robert's experiment proved that three simple habits can change how you feel by changing the neurology of your brain. And he showed that we can all do this by a simple process of repetition. It really is that easy. So now I'm going to show you exactly how to use those three techniques. By the way, some people think they can just read about these techniques and get the benefit. Of course, if you want to really increase your happiness you have to use these techniques exactly as I have written them. To change your life for the better, please start right now.

The Effect of Smiling and Laughing

Whenever you smile, you release serotonin, which is a neurotransmitter that makes you feel good. It may seem ridiculously simple, but people who smile and people who are smiled at both report that they feel happier. The serotonin is a signal from our body that lets us know something good is going on.

The more you smile at others, the more they smile at you. Once it becomes a habit to be smiley, it adds a steady stream of happy moments to your life and it helps you to permanently raise your overall levels of happiness.

Laughter also releases serotonin and endorphins. Research has shown that it boosts the immune system and helps the body to clear out toxins. That means that by laughing a lot you will have better digestion, fewer colds, and less flu. The key for us, however, is that your body releases neurochemicals that make you feel good.

Robert found that his subjects didn't even have to have anything to laugh about to get started. They could just pretend to find something funny to get going and just laugh for no reason at all, and it still had the same effect.

MAGICAL HABIT 1: SMILE AND LAUGH

Laugh 20 times a day.

Smile 40 times a day.

The Miracle Effects of Physical Exercise

The scientific evidence is overwhelming: Happy people are more active than unhappy people. And active people are more happy than people who get no exercise. That seems like common sense. After all, we have muscles that have evolved to be used. But it is more than common sense. As we have seen, the mind and body are intimately connected. Exercise stimulates your body to produce two chemicals that change how you feel. As you start to use your muscles, adrenaline is released, which increases your alertness and triggers the release of energy. Then when you finish exercising, endorphins are released, which give you a sweet, soft feeling in your muscles and a sensation of satisfaction and relaxation.

Exercise clears out all the stress chemicals from your body and rebalances your neurology and body chemistry. It physically changes the state of your mind and body and releases chemicals that make you feel good. Exercise even makes you sleep better. And exercise has been proved to be the single most effective treatment for depression. So when you get into the habit of exercising every day, it gives you a reliable base of good feelings to support your happiness.

But exercise does not mean you have to go to the gym, run on a track, or pump iron. Exercise is any movement of your body. Walking is one of the best forms of exercise.

You are already exercising with every movement you make during the day. So doing more exercise is simply a matter of doing a bit more movement. When I was developing my Weight Loss program I checked on the precise amount of exercise people were doing. Researchers found that the difference between an overweight person and a naturally thin person was just 2,000 steps a day. That's a 15-minute walk.

Going to the gym is fine, but I think it is far better just to build a bit of exercise into your life. Interestingly, some recent research has shown that exercise has a more beneficial effect on your mood when you do it in a natural environment. The research showed that people who exercised outdoors in a natural, green environment had a rapid boost in mood and self-esteem.

Whatever your current level of fitness, you can gradually and safely increase the amount of exercise you do until you regularly enjoy a good physical workout several times a week. It could be cycling, swimming, playing sports, or just walking. Anything that warms you up, gets you breathing deeply, and gets your heart beating faster will definitely change your mood. If you do it in a park or the countryside, that's a bonus that will lift your mood even further. And a by-product is that you will also be fitter, which is good for your health.

MAGICAL HABIT 2: EXERCISE

Do at least 20 minutes of exercise every day.

Whenever you have the chance, take your exercise outdoors in a natural environment.

Magic Dots

Little dots can change your life. Robert asked his subjects to stick little colored dots all around their house and their workplace, for example on the mirror, on the fridge, on the bathroom door, and in the hall.

Whenever they saw a dot, they had to think a positive thought. Here is an easy way for you to do exactly that and make it a really powerful force in your life.

This exercise has a very powerful effect because it does not try to stop you thinking about anything, you just repeatedly *add into* your life a strongly positive experience.

MAGICAL HABIT 3: SPOT THE DOTS

1. Stick at least a dozen colored dots around your home where you will see them as you go about your daily life.

2. Make a list:

   - three happy memories

   - three people you love or who love you, and

   - three things that could make you happy in the future

     If you find it difficult to find or remember three things for each category, make up some situations or possibilities that would make you happy.

3. Imagine or remember each item as vividly as possible. For each memory, in your mind's eye see it as if you are in the situation, hear what you heard, and feel what you felt just like you are back there again now. For each person, imagine being with them, hearing them, and feeling how good they make you feel. For each situation in the future, imagine it happening—see it, hear it, and feel it as though it is happening now. Take as much time as you need, right now, to work through your list. Notice how good you feel at the end. As you do this more and more it has a cumulative effect and you will start to feel amazing!

4. Whenever you see a colored dot, think of one of the items on your list.

Faster, Stronger, Deeper Change

Robert's three exercises produced a physically measurable effect in one month. We can make that change
faster and more powerful by working on other habits as
well. You don't have to do all of these exercises at once.
However, when you've practiced each one every day for
three weeks it will become automatic, so you can then
start to practice the next one.

Habits of Thinking

I have met so many people who desperately want to be happier or thinner or more confident but have habits that are actually maintaining the state they are trying to escape. This is because habits of thinking, behavior, and posture strongly reinforce certain feelings, regardless of our intentions.

For example, many depressed people say negative things to themselves over and over again. They say things like, "Oh God, I've got another day to get through" and "I'm going to be on my own again." As soon as things start going right they ask themselves, "When will it go wrong?" I have found that the effect of this thinking can be dramatically changed when we simply add a positive thought on to the end of a negative one. The next exercise shows exactly how to do that.

ADDING THE POSITIVE

Read the whole exercise through before you start.

- 1. Use the same vivid positive memories that you use when you see a colored dot.

- 2. Look out for any statements or judgments in your internal dialogue that make you feel sad, hopeless, or unhappy.

- 3. Whenever you hear one of those negative statements, add on to it "AND NOW I REMEMBER . . ." or "AND NOW I LOVE . . ." or "AND IN THE FUTURE . . ." and then bring to mind one of the items on your list. For example, you might have a thought like "I've got another day to get through" and add on, "and now I'm thinking how much fun I have with my best friend."

This exercise has a very powerful effect because you do not try to stop thinking about anything, you just *add on,* as soon as you can, a strongly positive experience.

When you use this exercise repeatedly, over and over again, you will discover that your brain begins to streamline the process so that as soon as the habit of negative thinking begins, it fast-forwards to the positive idea and feeling. In the end that makes the negative thought just like a colored dot: it becomes a signal to think a positive thought.

Black-and-White or Color

The language we use strongly affects our experience. It is like a stream of hypnotic suggestions. If you had someone staying in your house who commented negatively on everything, you would ask them to leave. Just because you need an internal voice to think with, you don't have to put up with it speaking negatively.

A negative language habit is thinking in black-and-white all the time, in which everything is labeled good or bad. Some matters are black-and-white but we don't need a permanent negative extreme. Some people think it doesn't matter if we exaggerate or use negative language as a joke, but even in jest black-and-white thinking is limiting. Negative thinking effectively shuts the door on positive possibilities. It rules them out so that our imagination doesn't even begin to think of them. And that stops us from creating the pictures and sounds in our head that are associated with those positive possibilities.

For example, it is not unusual to hear someone say, "Everything always goes wrong for me!" That person is having a bad day and they are expressing their frustration, but it is not literally true. They don't drop everything they hold, they don't fall over every time they try to walk, and they don't lose their wallet every time they go outdoors.

Some things work and some things don't. But if that person keeps saying negative phrases like, "Nothing works for me!" and "I never have any luck" they paint all the world black and they will not notice hundreds of possible happy moments every day.

Here is how to change black-and-white thinking and make room for happiness in your language.

HAPPY THINKING

Read the whole exercise through before you start.

1. Pay attention to your internal dialogue—the voice you use inside your head to think with.

2. Look out for words like "can't," "nothing," "always," "only," "every," "no one," and "never."

3. If you hear any of these words, repeat the sentence in your head and notice if that thought makes you feel bad or limited.

4. If so, change it from a general statement to a particular one. For example, turn "No one understands me" into "Bill did not understand what I said this morning."

5. Now check that there is room for a positive outcome in what you have just said. For example, "I will talk to Bill later and this time I will check that he has understood what I said."

The wonderful thing about these changes you can make to your everyday habits is that they can work for anyone, anywhere. Small habits practiced regularly produce great results. As we shall see later, some of us do have significant issues that lie beneath our unhappiness and we do need to address those issues. But even before we do that, by using these exercises to change our everyday habits we can begin to experience a measurable improvement in our lives.

Some of these changes are so simple and yet so powerful that it is difficult to grasp just how great the effect can be. The best way to find out is actually to make the changes and feel the effects getting stronger every day.

I have had some clients who repeated the exercises in this chapter for several weeks until they found they could rely on feeling happy every day. It doesn't matter how long it takes. If you practice each day your happiness will increase.

When the basic good feelings become a habit then you will find that the rest of the book is easier to understand and the exercises are easier to do. The more you practice the techniques, the more you will get out of each section of the book.

CHAPTER 4

•

New Routes
to Happiness

New Routes to Happiness

Feeling good is a great basis on which to build your happiness, but happiness is not "being up" all the time. There are all sorts of different types of happiness, or, to put it another way, we can have an overall feeling of happiness while feeling all sorts of different emotions. You can be excited and happy, or calm and happy. You could be happy running a marathon, happy lying on a beach, or happy making a cup of coffee. You can be happy even though you don't look happy.

The common misconception that happiness is "being up" all the time is magnified by all the media images that surround us and use laughing, smiling people as a visual shorthand for satisfaction. But that sort of enthusiastic, obvious happiness is just one type of happiness, and it can turn into a strange sort of trap. Some people even seem to use it to avoid all their other feelings.

I know several people who have been in motivational seminars and had a really powerful boost to their spirits. They learned all the techniques for being positive all day long. You could even ring them up in the middle of the night and they'd be enthusiastic and positive. But sooner or later, they'd feel down again. Then they felt cheated.

In real life we must have room for the whole range of feelings, not least because, as we shall see later, even uncomfortable feelings are valuable.

Pretending to be happy is like telling a "white lie"—saying something that is not true but with good intentions. There are times when it is a good and kind thing to do. The same is true of pretending to be happy. It can even "kick-start" real happiness—just like pretending to laugh can make you really laugh. But pretending all the time would be like lying all the time. People who do that begin to lose track of their real feelings.

The trouble with pretending is that we have to have an idea of the sort of happiness we want in order to fake it. But real happiness is full of surprises. We find ourselves feeling rewarded and fulfilled in ways that we didn't imagine.

Burn Out

I've worked with a number of high achievers recently who have everything in a material sense but their happiness levels were going up and down like a roller coaster. I know what it's like, I've done it myself. It is caused by being relentlessly driven to achieve and sometimes it's to avoid having any uncomfortable feelings.

They work until they burn themselves out and then they get down because they are depleting their vital neurotransmitters. Their body forces them to take a break by making them unwell.

They are treating life like a series of sprints rather than a marathon.

Two straightforward principles made a huge difference to their lives:

1. Listen to your body, and when it tells you to slow down, take a rest. Resting just before you are totally exhausted means your stamina overall will be stronger.

2. When you have a lot to do, create an A, B, C list.

   A *is essential and must be done today.*

   B *is important but can wait.*

   C *is everything else.*

   Just focus on A, then do as much of B and C as you feel like.

Sometimes just one problem feels overwhelming. My friend Kevin Laye created the following amazing technique that instantly helps you to feel differently about any problem. It recodes the way the brain is processing the information so that you can handle it from a more resourceful position.

STATUE OF LIBERTY

Read the whole exercise through before you start.

1. Think of the problem or issue that is bothering you. Make a picture in your imagination that represents it.

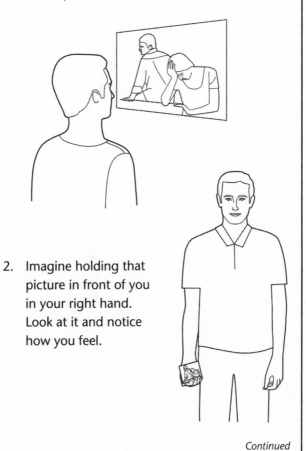

2. Imagine holding that picture in front of you in your right hand. Look at it and notice how you feel.

Continued

3. Now, still holding that picture, raise your right hand up so that you are standing like the Statue of Liberty and you are holding that problem high up in the air.

4. Now look at the picture up there and notice how different you feel. The situation is the same but the strength of the feeling is reduced because you are stimulating the brain waves associated with peace and comfort.

Recharging

As we saw earlier, happiness is not a fixed state of permanent elation. It is about having a background of rich contentment to your feelings and having more and more moments of joy alongside the usual daily feelings and challenges. This next technique will help you tune in to real happiness every day. People often tell me that when they do this, it shows them how much beauty and goodness is present in everyday life.

Often when I take people through this exercise they have a euphoric experience and they get insights about themselves and their life. Afterwards you will find people are more lovable, the world looks somehow brighter, more friendly, and full of more exciting possibilities.

This exercise is not about creating a once-in-a-lifetime high. It is about resetting your perspective on life, bringing a deep happiness to everyday life, finding joy in ordinary events, and automatically getting up in the morning and feeling happy to be alive.

HIGHER POTENTIAL

Read the whole exercise through before you start.

1. Choose somewhere to sit quietly for five minutes. Spend a little time, a minute or so, gently relaxing. Pay attention to your breathing. Imagine there is a silver thread coming down from the sky that is gently pulling you up from the very top of your head. Imagine letting that thread hold your head upright, let your shoulders drop and imagine you are supported by that silver thread.

2. Now let your imagination explore how you would be if you were fulfilling your highest potential. Imagine in front of you a screen, and, on it, watch a super-realistic movie of yourself in the best possible state going about your everyday life. Watch yourself being capable, kind, generous, balanced, and in control.

3. As you watch that movie, ask yourself, "If I were being loved, unconditionally, right now, how would that feel? How good can I feel if I am full of energy, if I were loved so much I could love as much as I can, if I had overcome the obstacles I face, if I had received so much that I could be as generous as I wanted?" If you were the best version of yourself, your highest potential, how would

Continued

you be, move, breathe, smile, think, act, deal with people, deal with difficult situations, how much joy would you feel in your body, what kinds of positive thoughts would fill your head?

4. Now float over into yourself in that movie so you see, hear, and feel everything from within your higher self with this wonderful feeling. Notice how good you can feel at your most loving, most confident, most generous, and most kind, just being relaxed and comfortable in yourself.

5. Really enjoy exploring how good this feels. Now spread this feeling through the whole of your body and heart and mind. Notice whatever lets you truly enjoy being totally at ease and free to love and appreciate your life completely. Notice the balance of peacefulness and energy.

6. Now look ahead and imagine how things will be keeping this feeling within you as you go into the familiar situations of your daily life. What is your home life like with all the love and generosity and wisdom of your highest potential? How do you feel as you wake up in the morning, as you meet people and go about your daily tasks? How will your work be different as you feel this comfortable, balanced, and capable? How will your evenings be different with this internal peace, love, and energy?

Continued

7. Now look ahead to at least three ordinary situations from your daily life over the coming week and vividly imagine how they will be when you are transformed by this inner connection to energy, balance, and happiness.

8. Keep this feeling with you throughout your day.

This exercise reinforces your new brain chemistry, and each time you do it, you introduce a greater capacity for happiness and reset your base of happiness to a higher level.

Choice

People get unhappy when they feel stuck in a situation that can't be changed. They may have difficulties like debts or housing problems or sharing their living space with a difficult partner or challenging children. It looks as though circumstances can completely prevent them from making the changes they want.

When people come to work with me, whatever their circumstances, I always tell them, "You have a choice." "What do you mean?" they say. "I can choose my debts to disappear? I can choose my children to behave differently? I can choose to be married to a film star?" And I say, "Whatever you think won't change the facts, but you can change your attitude towards those facts."

You can't always get other people to do what you want and you can't choose to be married to someone you have never met. We can't control everything that happens to us but we do have a lot of control over our thoughts, feelings, and choices. In other words, you can choose how you respond to what happens.

Every choice is a decision. Whatever your circumstances, you are in charge of what you do next and what you focus on. In fact, not only do you have the power to make choices, you make and take decisions all day long. You choose to get up or sit down. You choose to walk or take the bus. You choose to speak or remain silent, and even now you are choosing to continue to read this book rather than put it down.

Even if you put off a decision or refuse to make a decision or do nothing at all, you are *choosing* to put off a decision or refuse to make a decision or do nothing at all. We cannot avoid choosing, and at every moment the choices we make either move us towards our goals and values or away from them.

Amazingly, some of the most powerful choices we can make are about very, very small actions.

In the 1950s when racial segregation was prevalent in the United States, a remarkable African-American woman called Rosa Parks changed the destiny of the whole country. She refused to give up her seat on a bus for a white passenger. Her actions sparked off a bus boycott that led eventually to a Supreme Court ruling that Alabama's racial segregation was unconstitutional.

Everything we do in our lives is determined by our choices. Of course, some people are born with advantages, but there are plenty of people who have achieved extraordinary things against the odds because they made decisions that dramatically changed their lives for the better. You can choose to move towards a happier life right now.

Plenty of people say that they would like things to get better, but that's just stating a preference. That's like saying, "I would like to have a big house, a fancy car, and a fabulous lover" but not doing anything about it.

For your choices to have power you need to put commitment behind them and that means that you do whatever it takes, no matter what occurs, no matter what doubts you have. I am certain that during the course of reading this book you will have doubts that the system can help you. You will have reasons why you can't do the techniques, but it's your choices that will determine the quality of your life.

In one scientific study a thousand people were asked, "If nothing in your life changed, could you still be happier?" The result was fascinating: 95 percent of people said yes. This tells us one really important thing:

You can choose happiness.

People who have not cultivated the habit of making decisions do not realize how much power they have. But choice is not something that's only available to a select few. You don't need to take a course in choosing. Everyone has the power of choice. It can change every part of your life, your energy levels, your career, your relationships, your health, your income, your emotional well-being, and your happiness.

Your capacity for choice is an awesome power within you that no one can take away. Even if you were locked up you could still choose how you think and how you feel. You can change your destiny with a choice.

Choosing More

If you do anything repeatedly for several days you will be different. One of the most powerful, life-enhancing choices you can make today is to do the exercises in this book and do them over and over again. The scientific research is overwhelming: if you relentlessly force yourself to think about positive things you will change your brain chemistry and neurological functioning so that you cannot help but feel good more and more of the time.

However, I know there are people who find it difficult to make some choices even when they know they would benefit from them. They procrastinate. Procrastination can look like laziness but I found that when I worked with people who were putting off the moment of choice they were doing it just because they were frightened of making the wrong decision. They weren't lazy, they were scared. They also imagined they had to get it right the first time.

But you don't have to get it right the first time. The more choices you make, the better you get at choosing.

If you are not used to making big choices and decisions, start with some small ones. If you have a secret wish to make a really big change in your life, don't try to do something enormous right away. Instead, ask yourself what is the smallest thing you can do today that will take you one step closer to your goal. For example, if you dream of starting your own business you will need to have some capital, so you could put aside some money, even if it is only a dollar, towards your start-up fund. If you dream of performing on television you will need to build up your confidence in public, so you could take one more step towards being more confident with strangers, for example by talking to someone on the bus or volunteering to help out at an event.

Upside and Downside

Say, for example, I want to ask someone out on a date. What will happen if I ask and they say no? I might feel rejected or embarrassed for half an hour. How bad could that be? Say down 3 out of a possible 10. If on the other hand they say yes, that could be the beginning of a fabulous relationship: up 10 out of 10. It is a risk worth taking.

Whatever sort of choice you make, the next technique will help you in two ways. Firstly it helps you make sure your choice is one that will reward you, and secondly it makes the choice easier to carry out because it helps you see it in proportion.

MAKING GOOD CHOICES

Read the whole exercise through before you start.

1. Think about the choice you are considering.

2. On a scale from 1 to 10, how much good will come if you make this choice and everything works out well?

3. On a scale from 1 to 10, how much of a negative impact would you experience if you don't make this choice or if it doesn't work out?

4. If the answer to 2 is bigger than the answer to 3 it is clear you should go for it. If the second number is bigger than the first, it's probably best to find another way to proceed!

5. If the numbers are the same, ask yourself, "What is the smallest, easiest thing I can do to increase the upside?" If you can find an answer to that, do it and then make your choice. If you can't then just ask yourself, "Do I want to take this risk today?" If you don't, ask the question again tomorrow and see what has changed.

Now you know what to do, go for it!

CHAPTER 5

•

The Power
of Perspective

The Power of Perspective

We all live on the same planet and we all use the same five senses, so it is easy to assume that we all see the world the same way. Our own point of view is the most familiar thing there is. We all think we see things just the way they are. But we don't. We each perceive the world differently because we all understand the world on the basis of our own unique personal history.

All day long our mind is judging, commenting, and reacting to everything we perceive. In fact, we perceive the world by interpreting it. We don't first see lines and colors and then make a picture of the world. We perceive by recognizing patterns in what we see and hear and feel. Even our emotional reactions are shaped by patterns we inherit. In other words:

**Our past forms the lens through
which we see the present.**

That means it is not possible to see things without some kind of interpretation. The way we see things and the way we remember and think about things directly affects how we feel. So in this chapter I'm going to show you how to make some simple changes that will have a huge effect on your mood.

Objectivity

The importance of science has led people to think that "objectivity" is the best way to see the world. See the facts without any feelings. However, from a human point of view, objectivity is just another attitude. It is an interpretation that deliberately ignores our feelings. That is very useful to ensure that scientific measurements are taken accurately and so on, but as far as life is concerned it is a bit like turning the color off on your TV so you see everything in black and white and then saying that is more truthful. It is not more truthful, it is just a filter that reduces the richness of life. When you turn down the feelings, you also turn down the possibility of enjoyment.

Framing

There is no absolutely fixed meaning to anything in life. It is always affected by the point of view you bring. The way you make sense of the world, the meaning you bring to what you see, is a function of the point of view, or frame, in which you see things. One of the secrets of maintaining happiness is to use your frame to make sure that in difficult times you always stay in touch with the source of your happiness.

Over the years I have had the opportunity to work with people who have undergone some terrible tragedies, but their frame gave them an amazing strength that enabled them to handle them. Equally I have seen some people devastated by a relatively small challenge. The difference was in the way they framed these situations in their minds. The meaning in any situation depends on what we include or exclude from our frame of perception.

It is the same as the way a photographer uses framing to tell you what is important in a picture. He chooses his proportions, his point of view, and his angle so that the eye naturally travels to the elements he wants you to notice.

Many modern therapists use the art of "reframing" to help people to reinterpret problems and find solutions by changing the way they are framed in their perception. The ability to reframe our experiences gives us more choices; it makes us more functional and powerful.

When I worked with high achievers, I noticed that when something that other people would consider "terrible" happened to them, the high achievers say to themselves something like, "How does this help me?" Now, in order to answer this question you have to look at the situation in a certain way and it puts the incident in a positive context. It is not a matter of "true" or "false," it is a matter of a point of view.

As you become better at the art of reframing you give yourself more choices. The more choices you have, the more flexible you are. And the more flexible you are, the wider your range of potential responses. As systems theory says, whoever has the widest repertoire of actions is the most likely to have most control of the situation.

Controlling the frame through which you view the world is one of the most powerful ways to liberate your mind from unhappiness. For example, I might feel very stressed because I have lots of work to do today. If my frame is only today, all I can see is stress. But if I see today in the context of where I have come from and where I am going I can see it differently. I remember the happiness I felt when I worked hard and achieved my goals in the past and I look forward to the happiness I will feel when I have completed this work.

Filters

Every possible way of seeing the world is like a type of lens or filter. If we had no lens at all we simply would not see the world. However, some lenses and filters are more useful and comfortable than others. I have found unhappy people have views of the world that are limiting their capacity for happiness. It is a bit like someone who wears very dark sunglasses all the time. They complain that everything is a bit dim, dull, and dark. Occasionally in very bright sunlight things look okay, but mostly life looks grim. It is important to realize that they are not lying. And they are not deliberately making life difficult. They have just worn those glasses for so long that they've forgotten they're wearing them.

Other people feel like they are doing fine most of the time, then suddenly life feels grim for no apparent reason. That's like someone has randomly swapped their ordinary glasses for dark glasses.

If it turns out that you have been wearing dark glasses some of the time, or all of the time, I'm going to show you how to take them off and how to make a pair of spectacles that shows you the world in bright, brilliant colors and perfect focus.

Thought Experiments

In this chapter we will look at how to adjust how you think and imagine to bring out the best possibilities. Listening to the hypnotic trance we will reinforce those changes and generalize them throughout your life, and the profound relaxation of Big Mind will allow them to sink deep into your unconscious mind.

We are about to do a number of thought experiments that will change the way you feel. You will be reprogramming your mind like a computer. Please do all of the exercises now.

Sounds

We think, plan, imagine, and remember by making pictures and sounds in our heads. We use a copy of our own voice in our imagination when we rehearse things to say, and sometimes when we read. We talk to ourselves when we are planning or commenting or wondering. We use this voice all the time, day in day out, but most of the time we don't realize how influential that voice can be. Everything it says and the way it says it has an effect on how we feel and the possibilities we see. It is almost like having a hypnotist between your ears.

You can use that voice to radically change your mood. You can think exactly the same thoughts, with exactly the same words, and yet make changes that will transform your experience. Here's how.

USING THE INTERNAL VOICE

Read this exercise through before you start.

1. Think of something you say about yourself that makes you unhappy. It may be something someone said to you years ago or it may be a negative judgment you repeat when you feel bad.

2. Repeat the same phrase to yourself and notice how you feel.

3. Now notice where you imagine hearing that voice. Is it in your head or neck or chest? Is it towards the front or the back? Is it above your head or to one side?

4. Now, *repeating exactly the same words,* imagine floating that voice out of your body so it is 12 feet away on the other side of the room. Notice how different it feels out there.

5. Now hear the same words but in the voice of Mickey Mouse.

6. Keep replaying the words over and over again from the other side of the room in the voice of Mickey Mouse.

Continued

7. Now choose three more phrases that made
    you feel bad in the past and run it through
    all of these steps until you can hear the
    words as if they are on the other side of the
    room in a different tone of voice so you feel
    perfectly fine as you hear them.

When you do this three times, it establishes
a pattern that your unconscious mind can learn.
When you listen to the hypnotic trance we will
reinforce this process at an unconscious level to
remove the negative thoughts that you had been
repeating from the past.

You can also do it as many more times as you
wish with any negative phrases you want to clear
out of your mind.

Pictures

When we remember people and places we create pictures in our minds. For example, I'd like you to answer this question: "What color is your front door?" To get the answer you call to mind a picture of your front door as though you were standing in front of it. You see the door and you might even imagine putting your key in the lock. Seeing the door in your imagination is called visualization. All of us do it thousands of times a day, and we are so used to it we scarcely notice we are doing it. The pictures we make are not as realistic as how we see the real world, so we don't confuse them with reality, but they represent reality in our minds. Some people naturally make vivid pictures, other people naturally make plainer ones, but we can all do it.

The amazing fact is that the way we make those pictures has a huge impact.

Quite simply, how you make pictures in your imagination significantly affects how you feel.

The Movies of Our Mind

A useful way to think about this is to compare our experience to a movie. Think for a moment about how a movie is made. There are cameramen, lighting designers, set designers, costume designers, sound technicians, scriptwriters, composers, actors, editors, and directors all working for months and months to produce just a hundred minutes of action. Every part of each shot has to be set up to tell the story and deliver the mood the director has chosen. Everything is significant, from the costumes to the camera angle, from the speed of the action to the soundtrack. If you change just one thing the whole mood can change. The choice of camera lens, the focus, and the lighting all affect how we feel about a scene before a word is spoken. It is so complicated that it can take years to develop a script, and a single shot can take a whole morning to set up, rehearse, light, and shoot.

One of the keys to happiness is the discovery that we can choose how to edit and direct our own lives. We are in charge of what we focus on, how we light it, how we frame it, and all the other variables. Changing those variables changes the meaning of what we see and the feelings we experience. Let's see how this works with a simple example.

CHANGING PICTURES

Read the whole exercise through before you start.

1. Think of a person who made you unhappy
    in the past. Imagine their face in front of
    you. Notice the uncomfortable feeling that
    person created in you.

2. Now, imagine moving the image off about
    12 feet away.

3. Now shrink the image of their face so it's
    small.

4. Now drain all the color out of the image so
    it's black-and-white.

5. Now make it transparent.

6. Now make it fade out and disappear.

7. Now notice how different you feel.

By changing these aspects of how you were
picturing things in your mind, you have altered the
emotional effect of that memory. You have changed
how you feel about that person now and you have
reduced the effect they can have on you in the
future. This is an example of you running your brain
rather than it running you.

Making these simple changes reduces the emotional impact of the images in our mind. The overall principle is this:

Images that are bigger, brighter, and bolder have greater emotional intensity than those that are duller, dimmer, and further away.

Now do this exercise **three more times** with three more pictures of people or situations that upset you in the past and change the variables until you feel freed from all the negative feelings.

Outside or Inside

There is one important principle in how we remember or imagine things that has a huge effect on their power. It's really important whether you remember or imagine the incident from *inside or outside*. Let me show you.

STEPPING OUT

Read the whole exercise through before you start.

1. Take a moment to think back and remember a time in the past when you were not happy.

2. In your mind's eye, see where you were when that happened. See the situation as if you are in it. See it as if you are looking around from your own exact point of view in the situation so you see what you saw and feel what you felt. Watch what is going on and notice how it makes you feel.

Continued

3. Now, freeze the action and float out of your-self and this unhappy time so you can see the back of your head and the situation like it is happening to someone else.

4. Now, move the image off about 12 feet away.

5. Now shrink the image until it's small.

6. Now drain all the color out of the image so it's black-and-white.

7. Now make it transparent.

8. Now make it fade out and disappear.

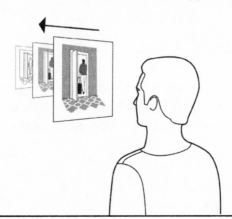

This single change makes an amazing difference to how you feel.

Being *inside* a memory intensifies the feeling.

Being *outside* a memory reduces the intensity of the feeling.

STEPPING IN

Read the whole exercise through before you start.

1. Think about something that would make you feel really happy and imagine watching a movie of it happening to you now.

2. Now float over and into the you in the movie. See through your eyes, hear through your ears, and feel how good it feels.

Continued

3. Now make the colors richer, brighter, and bolder, the sounds louder.

4. Notice what happens to the feelings.

Now let's bring all this together and use it to make a change to how you think and feel about yourself. The techniques at the end of this chapter let you leave behind all the negative or damaging labels that you have picked up in the past and opens the door to let happiness flood into every level of your life.

Labels and Stories

In our society we give people labels too easily. For example, so many people are labeled "depressive" now that depression is the fastest-growing disease in the Western world. Does that mean that thousands more people are more seriously depressed than ever before? Or does it mean that more and more people are experiencing sadness or difficulties or emotional challenges and are being given a label that defines them in a certain way? I suspect it is a bit of both. There may be very good reasons for saying a person is depressed at a certain time, but giving them a label makes it sound permanent. And if it is repeated enough, people take it on as an identity and build stories to support it.

Some labels and stories are positive, like "I'm good at math" or "I'm a loyal friend," but others are negative, like "I'm not very sociable" or "I'm not really a happy person."

And while there may be some truth in these stories some of the time, the more we tell ourselves these stories the more we believe them to be permanent. They are all just stories. Some of them support us and some of them don't. But they can be changed. Over the years I have seen so many people change because they didn't accept the stories other people told them and they changed the story they were telling themselves.

Einstein was told by his Greek teacher, "Nothing will ever become of you." After his first gig in Nashville, Tennessee, Elvis Presley was told by the owner of the venue, "You ain't going nowhere, son. You ought to go back to driving a truck." If Einstein had believed his teacher he would not have made the most important advances in physics in the 20th century. If Elvis had accepted that label, he would not have become the world's first global rock star.

Sometimes we hear a negative label so much that we begin to use it ourselves. As we hear more and more labels we weave them into the story that we tell ourselves.

A lot of people who tell me about their unhappiness begin by telling me their story about why they are different and they can't change. These are the sorts of things they were saying to themselves:

- I feel like I'm not meant to be happy.

- It is not worth trying to feel good because it will make me feel worse when I'm down again.

- The things I've experienced mean I can never be truly happy.

- We are all depressives in my family.

- My worries are far too real, I can't ignore them.

- I've always felt I don't fit in.

- Whatever I do, it won't make any difference.

What they didn't realize was that the story they were eager for me to believe was exactly what held them back from the changes they wanted to make.

Saying "I'm an unhappy person" is defining yourself by your past. That's like saying, "I can't run, because right now I'm standing still." If you define yourself by what you have done in the past, you will repeat the past.

All the things that were said to us, all the phrases we have repeated, and all the memories we have add up to a story we are telling ourselves. Some parts of that story are nourishing and empowering, and some parts of it bring us down. In the next exercise we are going to clear out all the negative pictures and labels and start to create positive, affirming pictures and statements that support happiness.

We will start this process right now, and it will be reinforced and continued when you listen to the hypnotic trance. All these positive pictures will be rendered even stronger by rooting them in the deep bliss of Big Mind.

CLEANING UP

*Read the whole exercise through before you start.
Now we are going to take all of the major
unhappy memories out of your mind and put them
on an imaginary wall of very small black-and-white
pictures and just before they disappear see them for
what they are . . . just thoughts.*

- Imagine all the unhappy times floating out of
  your head and on to a wall in front of you.

- Make the images small and black-and-white.

Continued

- See more and more of them appearing on the wall in front of you in black-and-white.

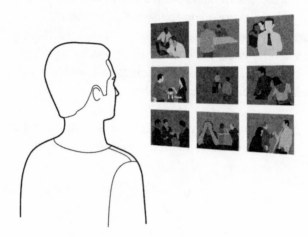

- Now look at them there and see them become more and more transparent before they fade out.

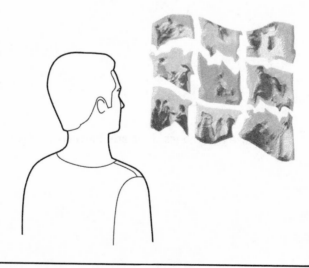

Amplifying Happiness

Now that we have cleared out all the negative imagery, we can build up the positive resources to sustain your happiness. In the next exercise you can use happy memories or you can imagine happy times. If you want, you can use a mixture of real times and imagined times. It doesn't matter if the situations are real or imaginary; the key is to follow the steps of the exercise so that whatever you are seeing or imagining amplifies your feelings of joy and resourcefulness.

STEPPING INTO THE NEW

Read the whole exercise through before you start.

- Remember or imagine a situation in which you feel really happy. Imagine looking around and seeing everything bright, clear, and colorful. Make sure all the voices you hear sound warm and friendly.

- Now make sure you are *inside* the scene— seeing things from your own point of view, hearing as though it is all here around you, and feeling all the good feelings.

- Now, keeping all these good feelings in this situation, imagine another situation in the future when you are going to feel even better, even happier, even more fulfilled. See that situation as if it is a movie in front of you and make sure you see it bright and clear and colorful. Notice how you look in that future scenario—see the confidence and warmth and happiness in your movements and posture, and the ease and kindness in your face.

- Now imagine stepping from the first scene into yourself into that even happier future and feel how good you feel.

- Let this feeling soak right into you so that you feel it from the center of your body to your skin, from the tip of your toes to the top of your head.

- Let the imagery fade now but keep this feeling with you and keep remembering it all day long.

CHAPTER 6

•

The Values of Happiness

The Values of Happiness

Happiness is not the same as pleasure. Pleasure is wonderful and I'm all in favor of it. It is great to enjoy a good meal, a hot bath, driving a new car, walking in the country, or admiring a beautiful sunset. We can get pleasure from all sorts of aspects of life. But pleasure on its own will not make you happy. If you do one pleasurable thing after another eventually you'll get bored. There is only so much chocolate you can eat. If one bar of chocolate is delicious, two bars are not twice as nice and a hundred bars of chocolate will make you sick. You would even get bored of caviar and champagne if that's all you had to eat and drink. If you only do things for pleasure, however refined or expensive, sooner or later you'll be left feeling, "Is this all there is?"

If happiness was determined by pleasure then the people with the most money would be the happiest people. Actually there are plenty of miserable millionaires. Once people can afford the very basics of life there is almost no correlation between wealth and happiness. In one study, researchers found that the richest people in America in the Fortune 500 were no happier than Masai tribesmen in East Africa.

I personally know plenty of people who have all the houses and possessions and toys and security that money can buy, and none of that makes them happier than other friends who earn a perfectly ordinary wage.

Happiness Is . . .

Happiness includes pleasure but it is different. Happiness is something deeper. Happiness is a backdrop to your life that makes everyday life rewarding; it gives you strength in hard times and it frees you to enjoy life fully at every opportunity.

The reason happiness seems difficult to define is because it is unique to each individual. There is no one thing or event that would make any person happy all the time.

For a baby, happiness is simple. It is created by love and comfort. Happiness comes easily to children because the world is fresh and new and exciting. As we grow up and explore the world, happiness is triggered by the joys of discovering the world and ourselves. In the first half of life we open up and explore. We make plenty of mistakes and learn from them, and we build up a bank of experience. As we develop our powers we find happiness in our achievements.

In the second half of life, we begin to bring together and integrate all that we have learned. In this way we get to know ourselves better. Eventually as we get a bit wiser we find happiness in self-realization and bringing happiness to others. Happiness arises from respecting your own highest values and deepest wishes. So what makes you happy is not fixed.

Happiness is relative to your own progress through life.

This explains why at certain times happiness can seem elusive. As we develop, how we find our happiness changes. However, each time we move on, our happiness becomes richer and deeper.

Goals and Values

When we are talking about happiness, it is important to see the difference between goals and values. Goals are like a compass; they help you set a direction for your life and help you to measure your success. Imagine you set yourself a goal: "In ten years' time, I want to own a house by the seaside." You could paint a nice, clear picture of what you want and become highly motivated. You will be very happy when you hit your goal—but it would be crazy to wait ten years to be happy. Goals should not limit your happiness.

Don't put off being happy until you reach your goals!

Whether you are close to your goals or far from them, you can be happy every day provided you are living your values.

Your values are the principles and states that you hold in the highest esteem. For some people it might be their religious beliefs, for others their families. You may have values like loyalty or integrity or career success. Your own happiness is founded in your own personal values. Values are what give meaning to your life.

I have worked with a number of people who were approaching the end of their lives and been privileged to learn from their insights. None of them looked back and wished they had had more money, more cars, or bigger houses. All of them were most grateful for the love of their families, for the beauties of the natural world, and for the joys of friendship. They all wished they had worried less and laughed more.

About 15 years ago I was sitting in a restaurant with a friend and he said, "We should meet here again in 30 years' time." That idea suddenly sent my imagination off into the future. I realized that in 30 years many of the people I knew and loved would have died. My body would be less fit. I would have been working on my career for another three decades. As these ideas rushed into my head, I remember thinking, "I'm going to love and appreciate my family and friends every day, because they won't all be here in thirty years' time. I'm going to appreciate my health and enjoy each day that I live." That conversation started me on a path towards realizing what I truly valued.

My own core values are love, laughter, loyalty, creativity, gratitude, and making a positive contribution to society. I build my life around those values and each day I ask myself these questions:

LOVE	**Am I expressing and receiving love?**
LAUGHTER	**Am I open to laughter and good humor?**
LOYALTY	**Am I being a good friend, and am I enjoying my friends?**

CREATIVITY   **Am I expressing and developing my talents?**

GRATITUDE   **Am I grateful for what I have been given?**

GENEROSITY   **Am I making a positive contribution to the world around me?**

I know that if I can check the "yes" box to all these questions every day, then I am living a happy life!

The next exercise will help you to do the same thing.

KNOWING YOUR VALUES

Read the whole exercise through before you start.

- Ask yourself, "What is most important to me?" For example, it could be your family, your career, fame, money, health, or relationships.

- Choose the five most important things in your life. Take each one in turn and ask yourself, "What is it about this that is important to me?" For example, if money is important to you, ask, "What is it about money that is important to me?" The answer might be "security" or "status." That would show that the values that are important to you are security and status. If family is important to you, ask, "What is important to me about family?" The answer might be "enjoying every day." Ask again, "What is important about that?" and the answer might be "love."

- Keep asking, "What is it about this that is important to me?" until you reach the value that drives it.

- Work through each of your most important things, and write a list of all the values that underpin them. These are your core values.

LIVING YOUR VALUES

Read the whole exercise through before you start.

1. Reread the list of your values.

2. Every day ask yourself, "How can I live my values today?"

3. If you have a decision to make, ask yourself, "What choice can I make that will most support my values?"

4. Make a note now to ask yourself three questions every day for the next week:

   (a) Have I lived by my values?

   (b) Has my life been enriched?

   (c) Do I need to adjust or add another value to my list?

Finally, we are going to rehearse living your values.

ENJOYING YOUR VALUES

Read the whole exercise through before you start.

- Think of the first of your values that springs to mind and remember or imagine a time when you were experiencing or living by that value, for example, being creative, or giving or receiving love.

- Vividly remember that time like you are back there again now. See what you saw, hear what you heard, feel how good you felt.

- Now go through that memory several times and as you experience the good feeling, press together the middle finger and thumb of one of your hands.

- Choose two more of your values, and one at a time experience the feelings associated with living those values, and press together your finger and thumb again.

- Now remember all three good feelings and press together your finger and thumb as you go through them several times and imagine taking those feelings into your everyday life, spreading them throughout your day.

What Can Go Wrong?

A lot of unhappiness is caused by people confusing pleasure with happiness. The boundaries got blurred at the beginning of the last century with the rise of consumerism. The consumer society has brought many benefits and technological advantages, but the cost has been the promotion of buying on the basis of desire rather than need. This has upset the natural balance of human feeling.

A hundred years ago fashion and brands were a very small part of the world of business. People bought things and used them. They would use them till they wore out. From a manufacturer's point of view, that meant there was a limit to how much product they could sell.

However, people like Edward Bernays, a nephew of Sigmund Freud, the founder of psychoanalysis, realized that if they attached feelings to products people would buy more than they actually needed. Bernays's insight paved the way for the advertising and branding industries.

Bernays made people feel they could buy more than just stuff. Buying things could give you status or make you cool. Bernays was brilliant at creating free publicity. He once sent a group of attractive models on a Women's Rights march and arranged for them to be photographed smoking in public. He told the press that it was a gesture of freedom as the women broke the taboo on being seen to smoke. In fact, he was promoting cigarettes for a tobacco company. The stunt worked and sales went up significantly.

Bernays helped people to buy feelings. There is nothing necessarily wrong with that. If you enjoy buying a new pair of jeans it is an easy way to feel good. But there is so much advertising around us now that it can be difficult to get away from it long enough to decide what you personally really want, as opposed to what someone else would like you to buy.

Shopping and Advertising

Advertising shouts at us from the television, from the roadside, on the Internet, on bus shelters, on tickets, and trains and airplanes. It sponsors our football teams and pays for radio stations and racing cars. It is all over the place. Advertising drives consumerism by continually persuading people to buy.

Shopping is now the number one leisure activity in the Western world. Advertising suggests that a watch, a car, or item of clothing will make you more sophisticated, elegant, and cool. This laundry detergent will make life easier, and that pizza will taste delicious. And why would you want this wonderful taste, or ease, or status, exclusivity, luxury, and comfort? Ultimately they are trying to persuade you that spending your money on their product will make you happier.

**Getting things may bring you pleasure,
but it may not make you happy.**

The same arguments are used for every sort of advertising, from hamburgers to houses. Eat this or live here and feel happier. Occasionally they are right. You buy the watch, car, or designer label and you do feel pleasure. It doesn't last forever, but you can tell that you feel better. Other times it doesn't really work. You win some, you lose some. It is great that we can all get pleasure from many of the things our society produces.

So the real problem is not that things don't make you happy, because sometimes you can really enjoy them. The problem with advertising is that it constantly urges us to look outside ourselves for stuff to make us feel good, so it trains your mind to want what you haven't got. Happiness, on the other hand, is nourished by noticing what you have got and appreciating it.

Happiness Is an Inside Job

Social researchers have measured happiness levels in Europe and the U.S. and they have shown that they have not increased since the 1940s. But in the 70 years since then we've had a vast increase in material wealth, we live longer, we have far better medical care, more communications, more art, and better housing. We have created a comfort-driven culture that has removed a great deal of hard work from our lives. And yet the research shows that we are no happier. It's clear that external circumstances do not determine happiness. In fact, researchers found that our external, material circumstances account for only 10 percent of our happiness.

The research shows that happiness comes not from things and people around us but from *how we respond* to the things and people around us. True happiness is an inside job.

It is easy to look at other people and other situations and imagine that we would be happy if we had what they had. But remember, the key to happiness is not what you have but how good you are at appreciating it.

**Don't compare the outside of someone else
with the inside of you.**

Retrain Your Brain

This exercise is a fantastically powerful way to retrain your brain. The consumer society sets us up with a feeling of continually lacking and wanting things. Advertising and media images continually show you things you don't have and attach good feelings to them. That trains your brain to crave what you haven't got. The fundamental search processes of the mind are continually looking for what we don't have, and as a result continually overlooking what we do have.

When you deliberately stop and repeatedly note what you do have and the good feelings that you can have, you can retrain your brain. When you practice any positive pattern of thought, you reinforce those neural pathways and change your brain chemistry. That means you can escape from all the desires and needs that are promoted by advertising and free yourself to focus on your own values.

A gratitude journal is an easy way to focus our attention on the good things we have. We always get more of what we focus on, so the more we focus on the good things, the more we attract them.

It is very simple to use. Just write down each day something for which you are grateful, such as your health, your family, a beautiful morning, a smile from a stranger, or a hug from a friend. Researchers have found that if you have to report to someone what you have done, you are far more likely to do it. In other words, what gets measured gets done. By writing this journal you are reporting what you are grateful for and telling your mind to look for all the good things in your life. That is like strengthening your happiness muscles.

You can keep your gratitude journal in a notebook, on a computer, or on a smartphone. To get you going I have started one page here, and at the back of the book is a journal for your first two weeks.

GRATITUDE JOURNAL

Today, I am grateful for . . .

1 ... *My health* ...

2 ... *A good night's sleep* ...

3 ... *The taste of my first cup of tea in the morning* ...

4 ... *The sunlight shining on the puddles in the road* ...

5 ...

6 ...

CHAPTER 7

•

Friends and Relationships

Friendship

When we are with other people, we are like radio stations transmitting our emotional state by means of thousands of little nonverbal signals in our posture, breathing, expression, and movement. At the same time as transmitting, we are also picking up other people's emotional signals. This means we literally sense each other even if we never actually touch each other at all. This is why friendship is such a rich source of happiness. When we are with friends who are warm and appreciative it feels good. We all like to be loved and appreciated. Mother Teresa said, "There is more hunger for love and appreciation in this world than for bread." The Dalai Lama has said, "My religion is kindness."

At another level, we increase our happiness by sharing our happiness. We are herd animals, so putting a smile on someone's face rewards the deep sense of community that is hardwired into us. Scientists have found that when we are in a group of people with something in common, the feeling of being in a herd causes a rise in our serotonin levels. Being kind or helpful or polite creates a sense of community, which is why we can feel good performing any act of kindness, whether to a close friend or to a stranger.

Some people are a bit wary of being too kind because they fear someone might take advantage of them. It is useful to remember that being kind does not mean you have to give things away. It doesn't cost anything to pay a compliment or to smile. When we do, we bring a good mood to the people around us because friendship and kindness are also catching. When we act kindly, all those thousands of nonverbal signals also show our kind intention, and people around us pick up those signals.

The only rule you need to remember is to be genuine. Feel kindness if you want to express it, and find something you really like about someone if you want to pay a compliment. Fake compliments are like counterfeit money. The more you use them, the more they get around and sooner or later you'll find them coming back to you.

If you are at loss to know what would be a kind way to behave, put yourself in the other person's shoes. Imagine seeing the world from their point of view.

If you saw a tourist looking lost, you could improve their view of your whole city by taking two minutes to give them directions or tell them about a good restaurant. If you are working with someone who is getting difficult and defensive, before giving them a hard time, step into their shoes and ask yourself, "What would help me feel better here? What does this person need to hear to feel appreciated and empowered?" Gandhi used this technique when negotiating with the British to achieve independence for India.

Sometimes just a smile makes all the difference. We are influenced by nonverbal signals all the time so we can't help feeling better every time we experience genuine kindness. That's why good things happen to you when you are happy. Generally other people are subliminally prompted to respond positively and feel happy around you, and your own good mood helps you see the positive possibilities in the people around you. When you feel good, the world looks good!

I was talking about all this with a colleague who realized that if he was nicer to all the people who worked for him they would be happier, more confident, and more productive. So he would get more out of them. He therefore quite cynically decided to act more friendly. As he was more friendly, people were more friendly to him and he admitted to me a few months later that he had ended up genuinely liking and appreciating them all and he was really grateful for all the friendship they showed him. He had become more loving and emotionally richer in spite of his selfish motives, just by actively being nice to other people.

This illustrates a fundamental principle of happiness:

If you want to have friends, be one to others.

The essence of friendship is not grand gestures, but kindness and caring. So being a friend does not mean helping everyone all the time or endlessly buying presents. It means small expressions of appreciation in everyday contexts. It is good to get into the habit of extending friendship with small random acts of kindness.

Boundaries

Happiness is a great creator of friendship; happy people make friends easily. There are no rules about how many friends you should have or need. Some people have lots of friends and some people are really happy with very few friends. Like attracts like, so happy people gather happy friends.

Friendship means being sensitive and open to your friends, but not insisting that they are immediately open back to you. It means respecting their differences of timing and interest. It means leaving the door open to friendship, not dragging people in. And occasionally, it even means closing the door.

Who Lifts Me Up and Who Brings Me Down

Unfortunately, "misery loves company," as the saying goes, so unhappiness can bring the wrong sort of friends into our life. Some people who are down just feel compelled to share their misery. People feel more secure when they share the same views as the people they are with. This holds true even if their views are making them unhappy, which is why unhappy people act as though they are trying to defend their unhappiness. They don't actually want to be unhappy—they just feel insecure if they let go of the beliefs they have gotten used to. They really do try to feel better, but they end up spending all their time talking about their problems.

In the end each of us has to make a personal decision to move away from unhappiness. You have decided to use this program to increase your happiness. You can't make anyone else do it. If they are not yet ready to make the necessary changes, you just have to stand back and let them join us in their own time.

Of course, a good friend will be there for you when you are down, and you would want to help your friends too. The friends we don't need are the ones who don't want to change their problems but just keep them going on and on and on. In the long term, they do need help, but endless sympathy won't help them or you.

It can be very difficult to pin down exactly what is going on, or what people are saying that is unhelpful, but there are three simple questions you can ask that will help you identify who are the friends you want to keep and who are the friends you want to leave behind.

For each of your friends, look back over the time you have known them and ask yourself these questions:

- Does this person take my energy up or do they take my energy down?

- After I have seen them, do I generally feel better or worse?

- Overall, do both of us feel happier and enriched by our friendship?

Here are some techniques that will help you deal with the people in your life who bring you down. Each of the techniques helps you to keep a healthy distance from people when and where you feel it is necessary. It is worth noting that doing this also helps you to be closer to someone if you choose. If you can be polite and firm and separate, it is also clearer when you invite someone to be close. As the old saying goes, "Good fences make good neighbors."

THREE BOUNDARIES TO CREATE A HEALTHY DISTANCE

Read the whole exercise through before you start.

1. Stay away

If someone consistently brings you right down, stay away from them. If at all possible, cut them out of your life entirely. You don't have to feel guilty about this because you have already tried to help them, and if the talk and all you've done was going to help, it would have done so by now. Strangely, when people are very needy or very down, they can only actually use a very little help. If you give them more than that, it simply goes to waste. Just let them go, and they may even find what they need in the space you create by leaving them.

2. "I can't decide right now, I'll get back to you"

A lot of difficulties in friendships arise because one person believes they have a good idea, and with enthusiasm or pleading or neediness they drag their friend into doing something the other person doesn't want. You don't want to get into an argument or a long discussion with these people, so practice saying these three phrases until they come to your lips automatically:

"I can't decide right now, I'll get back to you."
"So where does that leave you?"
"What's the best solution here for everyone?"

Continued

The other person may be caught up in a lot of plans or stories or ideas. What matters, however, is the outcome. These questions help you focus on that and decide what you really want. They will give you time to think, and if you really like the idea you can go back later and agree.

3. The shield of white light

If you find yourself in the company of people who you feel have taken advantage of you in the past, or who make you feel uneasy or drained, imagine a shield of white light surrounding you. Inside it is your space, protected by the light. Outside is the public space. If you want to let someone or something in you can choose to do so. Otherwise just imagine all their feelings and intentions and ideas being stopped by the shield. Then you can sense them, look at them, and think about them at your leisure and make your own reply in your own time. This works on two levels. Psychologically it creates an emotional boundary, and at a very subtle level the micromuscular movements of your nonverbal signaling will convey that you are safe, confident, and protected.

Whose Feeling Is It Anyway?

Sometimes the cause of our unhappiness is not even our own feelings. When I studied family systems theory, I saw that families dish out emotional jobs the way they dish out household chores. Just as one person does the cooking and someone else does the washing up, so it is the same with feelings. Usually there is one person in particular in a family who does the encouraging, one person does the nurturing, and so on.

However, if that person refuses to take on the responsibility of their emotional role, another one takes over the job. It reminded me of that party game for children called Hot Potato.

Family therapists have found that the same sort of behavior can happen in families and among groups of friends or colleagues. People have emotional tasks, but if they refuse them they can pass them on to other people. This is what we mean when we say that we feel as though someone just dumped their problems on us.

If you are feeling fine, then you meet someone and after you leave them you feel bad, it is a reasonable guess that the bad feeling came from them.

If you think that someone else has dumped their feelings on you, you can use this technique to free yourself. This exercise gets rid of feelings that don't belong to you. If the feelings really are yours, you can deal with them, and we'll look at that in the next chapter.

RETURN TO SENDER

Read the whole exercise through before you start.

1. Notice where you feel the bad feeling in your body.

2. Imagine a shape and a color for it.

3. Then imagine moving it out of your body and holding it in front of you.

4. Imagine wrapping it up like a parcel.

5. Now imagine launching it from a catapult with such force that it goes flying away over the horizon.

6. Notice how you feel. If there are any other leftover bits of feeling lying around, do the same again until you feel as comfortable as you like.

Close Relationships and Happiness

Psychologists have conducted research during the last 30 years to determine the factors that determine happiness. They tracked people over many years and they discovered that lots of happy people were in long-term relationships. Therefore, they concluded, long-term relationships make you happy. Some of the researchers even went so far as to say marriage makes you happy.

However, as they analyzed more data over more years they discovered that was not quite correct. It was not being in a long-term relationship, or being married, that made you happy. Actually, people who were happy attracted long-term relationships into their life. So it was not relationships that were making people happy, it was that happy people were making long-lasting relationships.

This finding was reinforced by a major study that ran over 16 years and showed that people who were happiest in their relationships were also happiest before they were even in the relationship. The consequence of this research is very clear.

Being happy in yourself is the best preparation for a happy long-term relationship.

Your Relationship with Yourself

When you are happy with yourself, someone else is more able to be happy with you. The basis of good relationships is a good relationship with yourself.

We can see why this is true if we imagine the situation from the point of view of your partner. If you are not at ease with yourself, you will be edgy and difficult to live with. That undermines your relationship.

So to relate well to others, you must relate well to yourself. That means you must have a good self-image, so when you think of yourself you have a positive and accepting attitude.

You must have confidence in yourself so that if you make a decision you are wholehearted and, if necessary, brave enough to follow it through. At the same time, you must be kind and sensitive enough to accept and respect your own vulnerabilities. Use the next exercise to improve all of these aspects of yourself.

This exercise can bring about the most wonderful transformation. It is not merely the best way to set yourself up for a healthy romantic relationship, but also if you are on your own or if you have recently split up with a partner, it is one of the most rewarding and healing things you can do. As we grow up, almost all of us suffer a few knocks and setbacks. Some of them can really hurt and if we don't know what to do with that hurt our psychological mechanism cuts it off. It is as though we disown a part of ourselves. This exercise helps to heal those wounds. It will be reinforced later on and during the trance and bliss of Big Mind on the hypnotic trance.

Some people told me at first that this exercise seemed a bit strange. They thought they would feel silly imagining talking to and holding their younger self, but every single one of the people who have used this exercise has told me how powerful it was. Strangely it was the people who felt most awkward about it at first who experienced the most powerful and profound changes.

Read this through carefully before you do it and then take as long as you need on each step to make sure you feel each part of it vividly and clearly.

HEALING YOUR YOUNGER SELF

Read the whole exercise through before you start.

1. Remember a time in the past, as long ago as you wish, when you were struggling or unhappy.

2. Picture the scene as an old black-and-white film on a TV screen and stop the action at the point where your younger self was feeling really bad.

Continued

3. Now imagine that, just like a special effect in a movie, you can float into the scene and speak directly to your younger self.

4. Tell your younger self that you are from the future and that everything is going to be fine.

5. Tell your younger self that you love them and value them completely.

Continued

6. Tell your younger self that you have survived, and anything else you know now about that situation that will help them feel better about it.

7. Now vividly imagine reaching out and comforting your younger self by embracing or holding them until you feel really warm and loving for your younger self and you sense that your younger self has felt and accepted your love and appreciation.

8. Finally, place your younger self in your heart so you can continue to feel that love.

Helping Others

When you have firm, fair boundaries and you are truly kind to yourself, you are in a great position to be kind and helpful to others. As you are happy in yourself there will be no hidden agenda in your relationships. You won't be trying to get other people to make you happy—you already are!

Happiness is a bit like love. The more you give it away the more you get. In fact, making other people happy is one of the simplest ways to make yourself happy. Sometimes all it takes is a smile or a kind word.

CHAPTER 8

•

The Value of
Emotions

The Value of Emotions

All of the exercises I have shown you so far have been tested over and over again and proven to work for thousands of people. If you have followed the instructions properly you will now be feeling much better on the surface and you will also be moving towards a much deeper sense of happiness based on your own personal values.

Nevertheless I know that some people will be skeptical or worried that they won't achieve the happiness they are seeking or that the changes they feel won't last.

It may be that you are one of those people who feels this isn't working properly for you. If so, read this chapter very carefully. If you are feeling fine and can sense your happiness getting stronger and stronger, you may find that you don't need to use these techniques right now, but it is a good idea to know about them so that you can use them in the future if necessary.

Feeling Stuck

I have worked with some people who have had real trouble maintaining the benefits they have achieved. In spite of all the work and testing that I had done, I was still finding people who somehow were not getting the permanent changes they wanted. There were also some people who found it strangely difficult to follow the instructions, even if they took them really slowly. When I found these few people who didn't seem to get or keep their positive changes, I obviously looked long and hard to find out what wasn't working.

Over-optimistic

There were some people who were just being over-optimistic. They practiced the exercises a couple of times, felt better, and left it at that. Naturally the results faded because they had not repeated the exercises often enough to ensure their new behavior was stronger than their old habits. They just needed to follow the instructions more carefully. Each exercise must be done for at least two weeks so you don't just feel happy for a moment but you establish the pattern that maintains your happiness.

Blocked

But there was another group who did work hard and practice and still it wasn't working. It was as though whatever they did, within a few hours or days the good feeling would be undermined.

They knew what I was talking about and they felt a bit of change but there was a sort of disconnection. When they did the exercises it was as though they were doing them with their head, but their feelings were behind a glass screen.

At the same time they had other feelings that seemed to keep coming back. And that was a bit disappointing because they had learned a great deal about how to change their state and feelings.

Emotions

So why were they feeling disappointed? There is so much you can do: You can change your posture, your internal voice, and the pictures you make in your mind's eye. You can bring wisdom and compassion into your relationship to yourself. You can lift yourself out of the bad moods and have more freedom than ever to enjoy yourself. Surely, it seemed, the secret to a happy life is just to change the pictures and sounds in your head and you can feel whatever you want.

However, that is only part of the story. Although we can change how we feel, we cannot totally override our emotions all the time. What is more, when you find out what they can do for you, you would not want to. Our emotions, including even our uncomfortable emotions, contain a treasure trove of reward and fulfillment that will deepen and enrich your happiness more than you can imagine.

Emotions are not just sensations that float around your life. They are part of our intelligence, just as much as thinking. We can change how we feel to a certain extent. We can reduce the intensity of feelings, we can get rid of unnecessary repetition, and we can remove feelings that are out of date, but we can't choose to have only the feelings we want. Our emotions are a form of perception.

> **Our emotions are signals. They are**
> **simply saying, "Pay attention to this."**

The feedback we get from our emotions is a natural and vital part of our existence. If we try to block our emotions, we block a channel of perception. That would be like walking around wearing a blindfold. And even though we might not want to listen to the emotion because it is uncomfortable, if you suppress it, it does not vanish. It goes away temporarily but it will come back again because it is still trying to deliver its message. It is like a postman trying to deliver a parcel. If you don't open the door, it will keep knocking on the door on and on and on. Then it will knock louder and louder and louder. An extreme example of this is the panic attack. A panic attack is irrational and out of proportion. Underneath it there is often just a simple message trying to get heard. It only got that big and scary because we were not willing or able to accept that emotion when it first tried to deliver its message.

Learning to handle our emotions and to understand them is as important as learning to use our minds to think clearly. Unfortunately, for the last 300 years Western culture has placed a lot of emphasis on suppressing emotions. Huge social forces like religion, revolution, drinking, drug taking, gambling, sex, and shopping have been used to avoid dealing with emotions. With all that surrounding us, most of us have a bit of catching up to do in order to truly benefit from the potential of our emotional wisdom.

Emotions Are Messages

Emotions have messages for us. If you are feeling bad, it is because there is something you need to notice about yourself, your environment, or your relationships. Our emotional intelligence is part of our animal nature. It reacts immediately to people and situations at an unconscious level. It reads all the nonverbal signals that tell us about physical and emotional threats and opportunities and, most importantly of all, it tells us how we are relating to ourselves. Emotions protect and guide us.

Our emotions are our friends.

Emotional pain is there to protect and guide us, just as physical pain teaches us not to hold our hands over a fire. However, sometimes we cannot escape from the source of emotional pain. For example, if we go through tough times as children, we may not have the emotional resources to deal with what we face, and if the feelings are too painful we cope by deliberately losing touch with them.

There are many reasons why people can lose touch with the part of themselves that knows immediately what they hold most dear and what matters most. If that happens it makes people unhappy. As we shall see, the secret of resolving the past and returning to our natural state of happiness is to learn how to hear and process our emotions, even if that means starting with the unhappy feelings.

Noise

Of course, not all of our feelings are important. Emotions vary just as much as thoughts. Some of our thoughts are simple, some are complicated. Some are repetitive and dull, some are important and insightful. It is the same with feelings. Some are simple, some are complicated. Some feelings are trivial, others are important and insightful. Sometimes feelings just get stuck in the same way that you can get a tune stuck in your head. They may mean nothing at all but they go on and on like a tape loop repeating the same bit of music over and over again. It is not always obvious if an emotion is carrying an important message. However, all the techniques work equally well to help you process your feelings whether they are meaningful or not. If there is a message to be delivered, they will help you receive it. If the feelings are just background noise, they will fade away.

Everyday Messages

We are all individuals and our emotions are very finely tuned responses to our unique circumstances. But there are some general themes that will help you begin to understand some of the most common emotional messages we receive on an almost daily basis:

ANGER is usually a sign that one of our rules or boundaries has been violated, either by ourselves or by someone else. The message is either to take action for what we believe is right or, in some cases, to accept the things we cannot change. Occasionally anger arises because we are frightened. Our body is making energy available to us, but as we don't know what to do it triggers the default action of defending ourselves. One of the most useful questions to ask at this point is, "What is the best solution for everyone here?" But of course if you are angry it is hard to be that calm. It is easiest to start by completing this sentence, either to yourself or out loud: "I am very angry because what I really want is . . ." That is easier to do and it focuses you on the positive intention of your anger. Once you know what you want it is a bit easier to then find out what other people are wanting.

FEAR is a warning that something bad *could* happen, so you'd better be prepared. If you feel that you are fully prepared, or if you are experiencing fear in a situation where you normally feel comfortable, it could be a genuine warning of physical danger. If there is no threat and the fear makes no sense, you will find that the exercise on page 150 will be very liberating.

FRUSTRATION arises when you're not achieving the results you want in the time frame you believe you should achieve them in. Sometimes frustration is like a slow-burn version of anger. The message is usually to clarify and reflect on what you want. Is something or someone else standing in your way, or do you have a conflicting need yourself that you have overlooked? When you've had a good look around, you can decide how best to revise your strategy or your goals.

GUILT tends to come about whenever you are not living up to a standard of conduct. The big question to ask about guilt is whether that standard really belongs to you or whether it was forced on you by your family or education. Very often guilt, and shame, arise not because we are really bad, but because we have been misled into failing to trust our own deepest values. The exercise on page 110 will help you realize your own values.

SADNESS is the result of feeling that something is missing from our lives, either because we've lost it or we've lost touch with it. Underneath every sadness there is a tenderness because we are only sad about something we have lost when we cared for it. Sadness reminds us to treasure what we have experienced and to be open to caring and loving in the future.

Stuck Feelings

A lot of unhappiness is the result of getting stuck halfway through a feeling. We might feel angry or sad or fearful or frustrated, but if we don't really pay attention to the feeling and try to push it away, it pushes back. The more we struggle trying to push away or deny our feelings, the more we suffer. An emotion with a message doesn't go away. It just continues to nag us, trying to deliver its message. Some people manage to push the emotions away most of the time. They work hard and play hard and keep themselves busy. Then when one day they are just too tired they pause, or take a holiday, and the emotion jumps right in again, still trying to get heard. That can be a shock, and can appear puzzling as the original cause of the emotion is way back in the past. In those cases it is really helpful to remember that ultimately our emotions are working for our own benefit, even when they start by feeling extremely painful.

Dynamic Range

People often think that because I teach and practice these techniques on a daily basis, I never feel bad or uncomfortable. While I do choose to feel good in most situations, I always take the time to feel my feelings and listen to any messages they may have for me. That means that, like everyone else, I too have to feel sad or painful feelings sometimes.

It is important to have a full dynamic range of feelings. For example, it is appropriate to experience grief if someone dies. The grief is there because they meant something to us. However, it is also important, in due course, to move on. No one who loved us would wish us to be in mourning for them forever. The important thing is to feel our emotions and accept whatever they bring up.

There is no such thing as a "negative" emotion. There are painful or uncomfortable emotions but they all have messages for us. If they are ignored they become more painful because they are still trying to deliver their message. If we don't know how to process them it can be like living with an elephant crashing around our lives creating chaos but never being acknowledged. We need to remember that, originally, all it was trying to do was to help us. The next exercise shows us how to receive that message.

Listening to Emotions

There are different ways of feeling, just like there are different ways of listening to music. We can pay attention to music or be half-listening or we can try to ignore it. We can just hear it, or try to analyze it, or let ourselves be moved by it or even sing along with it.

We can have all these different attitudes, and more, to our emotions. The most useful attitude we can have to our emotions is to feel them without judgment and without being overwhelmed.

As you read this you might notice you begin to feel some emotions and that is a signal that they are ready to talk to you. When an emotion delivers its message, we get an insight into ourselves and our attitudes or we find we can let go of a pressure to act or be in a certain way. You learn something more about yourself. This can be very, very simple—"I'm hurt" or "I'm angry"—or it can be more subtle, something like, "I care more deeply than I thought."

Listening to our emotions involves bringing to them our attention, our honesty, and our willingness to be open to change. This is called processing our emotions, and the next exercise takes you through it one step at a time.

PROCESSING EMOTIONS

Read the whole exercise through before you start.

1. Find a place where you can be quiet and undisturbed for 20 minutes.

2. Sit down and relax. Let your shoulders drop and your breathing become calmer and deeper.

3. Notice the movement of your breathing and feel your feet on the floor. Feeling your feet and your breathing protects you from being over-whelmed. Keep aware of your feet and your breathing throughout the rest of the exercise.

4. Now move your attention through your body scanning it from your toes to the top of your head and notice whatever physical feelings you have. For example, you might just feel a bit light-headed, or you may have tension in the pit of your stomach or maybe your legs feel very heavy. Whatever you feel, simply notice whatever it is without any judgment.

5. Now notice your emotional state. Is there any resistance to what you feel? Or is there some tension around your feeling like a fence trying to keep it under control? If there is any tension or resistance, very slowly and very gently allow it to relax. Allow your-self simply to witness whatever it is without suppressing it or turning away.

Continued

6. Let yourself wonder, "What is this emotion about?" or "Why do I feel like this?" Even if you think the answer is obvious, let yourself wonder about it a little.

7. Now notice whether you are saying anything in your mind that is connected to this feeling. Notice statements such as, "It's not worth it," "I miss my children," or "I don't know what to do about my debts." Notice the words, but do not react. Notice any pictures that come to mind. Just notice them, but do not react.

8. Still keeping aware of your feet and your breathing, notice any impulses that arise, such as wishing to ignore the emotion, to reject it, to blame someone, to despair, to drown it out, to dismiss it. Just notice all those reactions without responding to them.

9. Now that you have noticed the reactions all around the emotion, go back to the center of what you feel physically and emotionally. Let yourself be open to however this emotion moves you. If you want to cry, cry. If you want to laugh, laugh. Welcome any new thoughts or ideas that pop up.

10. Just sit with that emotion until you feel tired or bored or it has disappeared. When all the energy has gone from the experience you know that you have done enough for today, so you leave it there, have a stretch, and get on with life.

This exercise can sometimes be very undramatic. You witness what you feel and it passes. Other times you can be quite surprised to find out what you are really feeling when you give yourself the chance. Actually, our feelings are always at work within us and trying to help us—we just sometimes get unhappy because we don't make time for them. This exercise helps you to make that time.

It is valuable to do this exercise many times, whenever you notice you have a persistent uncomfortable emotion. Sometimes it takes you straight to an insight that changes your life in a moment. On other occasions you can get all the way to the end without really much change or understanding. If that happens, just leave it, and do it again next time that emotion is really present for you.

Stacked Emotions

Sometimes when you do this exercise you will find at the end that you have a completely different emotion.

For example, I had a client who told me he would fly into a rage with his girlfriend over the most trivial things. He had no idea why, but it kept happening over and over again. We went through the Processing Emotions exercise to find out more about his anger. At the end he was very surprised to discover that underneath it was fear. What was he frightened of, we asked. He found that he was frightened that he could never have a successful relationship. And why was he frightened? Because he felt he could never trust his partner. And why did he not trust his partner? Because he had been so hurt by the breakup of a previous relationship. He was angry because deep down he was still hurt. And he was hurt because he had loved someone. Underneath it all was love.

The emotion he did not really understand was at the top of a stack of emotions that at the bottom were triggered by his desire for love. In order to release him from that anger we went through the Processing Emotions exercise four times. We processed anger, fear, distrust, and hurt before we found the love.

Emotions can stack up in all sorts of different ways.

Another client had been so hurt as a child that she got angry. And the anger was so intense that she felt frightened she might lose her temper, lash out, and then be punished. That fear was so strong that she felt panicky. She didn't know how to cope with the panic so she just froze up and felt that she couldn't do anything at all. She couldn't shift that feeling and gradually became more and more anxious. When she came to see me she told me anxiety was making her unhappy, but she had no idea why she was anxious.

She went through the Processing Emotions exercise six times—once with anxiety, once with feeling frozen, once with feeling panicky, once with fear, once with anger, and once with the hurt. Underneath she found that she was much more sensitive than she had believed. As an adult now, she was capable of looking after her sensitivity.

All our emotions ultimately are trying to help us, and uncomfortable ones are just trying to warn us. We build up stacks of emotions just because at the time we first experienced them we were not able to react properly or to deal with what we felt. So another emotion arose in response to the first one and covered it up.

This process can carry on and on, feeling on top of feeling, layer after layer. Emotions are hidden one inside another like Russian dolls. Each time the next feeling takes us further away from the original feeling and the original cause, so we can end up with painful feelings that seem to make no sense at all.

We can use the Processing Emotions exercise to remove them, one at a time, so that we can understand what happened and find our way back to the positive intention of looking after yourself, which is at the bottom. I think of this exercise as like unblocking a pipe full of feelings. As we take them out and release them one at a time, the pipe is cleared so from now on you can receive your emotions and process them directly.

The hypnotic trance will also assist this process at the level of the unconscious mind. It doesn't matter whether there is one emotion or several; the process can carry on, one step at a time, until you are totally free of all the emotions that were blocked in the past.

It is really simple to process stacked emotions regardless of how many there are of them. I have outlined how to do this below. It is an extraordinary thing to discover that underneath your anxiety, anger, or fear is love.

PROCESSING STACKED EMOTIONS

Read the whole exercise through before you start.

- Go through the Processing Emotions exercise over and over again with each of the emotions you discover.

- Take a break between each time you run the exercise. That break can be any length that suits you. It can be a couple of minutes or a couple of weeks. There is no need to rush the process. You will find that each time you run it, you release a bit more of your emotional energy and you will feel lighter and happier.

- If at the end of processing an emotion you feel the new emotion is intense you can use the exercise (see pages 150–151) to reduce its intensity.

- You will know that you have reached the bottom of the stack when you find a feeling that is kind and loving to yourself.

The Miracle of Release

Occasionally people find really amazing changes are possible when their emotions are released and processed. Some time ago I saw a man who was a lawyer. He was married with three children and he commuted to work every day by train. He didn't really like his job and each day as he stood waiting on the platform he felt more depressed. When he found himself thinking about jumping under the train he decided to truly explore his depression. He didn't try to work it out with his head; he used a process very like the one I'm going to show you. When he let his depression talk to him, it told him he was frustrated because he was not expressing his creativity. When he looked into his despair, he found that one of his deepest values was not being expressed.

By the time he had finished the process he had quit his job, left an unhappy relationship, and gone to art school. None of that was easy, but he now enjoys his creative talent every day and is a very successful artist.

Benefits

This exercise is one of the most powerful ways we can transform the hurt or pain we have suffered in the past. As we finally clear that backlog of emotions there is a wonderful feeling of lightness and relief. As we let go of that pain, the energy involved in it is released and our natural happiness is strengthened and expanded.

Sometimes we find that the insights we get from this exercise are exciting and liberating. We can discover wonderful and surprising things about ourselves that have been buried beneath our painful feelings. We don't just discover how to be happier, we find new directions in life and a new, richer way of relating to people.

•

CHAPTER 9

Bringing It All Together

Bringing It All Together

It is a wonderful paradox that when we face and accept our most uncomfortable emotions we are freed to experience the deepest happiness. It is so unexpected! We are surrounded by so many messages promising unlimited satisfaction and entertainment and ways to avoid what we are feeling. Surely, it seems, if everyone else is doing it, it must be the right thing! Escapism is the biggest business in the world. But when we stop running away, we find that the deepest happiness and the most satisfying rewards come from caring for ourselves enough to love and accept our pain and vulnerability as well as our strength and virtues.

Avoidance

Nevertheless, for people with a backlog of painful feelings, avoidance is popular. Some people develop a whole lifestyle in which they avoid their feelings. They fill their time with work and relentless activity. If they are talented this can look like a very successful life.

Others drown out their emotions—temporarily at least—with a physical feeling. At the most extreme this is the basis of addictions, from eating disorders to drug abuse. The addictive activity, for example eating, drinking, taking drugs, or whatever, produces an absorbing physical sensation or psychological activity. Some people become addicted to healthy pursuits like being fitness fanatics or marathon runners.

If avoidance works we can keep these behaviors going for years, because we don't notice what we are running from. It is only when the addictive behavior itself becomes a problem that we need to turn and face our deeper feelings.

This book is not focused on recovering from addiction, but if people choose to do so, it is worth pointing out that even people with very serious addictions can recover completely. There are lots of good programs out there that can help people.

Denial

Another way to deal with emotions that are painful is to stop feeling them. Because our intellectual intelligence can work separately from our feelings, we can concentrate on doing things with our minds and keep our attention off the part of our feelings that is hurting. If we do this consistently for a long time, it becomes a habit and we just stop using that part of our feelings. It is as though we saw something horrible with our left eye and just closed the eye so we don't see it anymore. That works, but the penalty is that we don't have that eye available to see the rest of the world with. With our feelings it is the same. If we close down a part of them it helps us not to feel the pain, but we don't have that sensitivity available for the rest of our lives. The next exercise helps you to deal with any feeling and free up your emotional perception.

Difficult Feelings

Some people struggle to make sense of a vague feeling like being anxious or feeling depressed. And occasionally people are reluctant to process their emotions because they fear that something they really don't like may come out. So when they try to use the Processing Emotions exercise they find that they can't seem to get started or it doesn't really make sense at first.

The next exercise helps you to be with any emotion at all, no matter how vague or strong or weak, and to experience it safely. It helps you to transform your experience and receive the message of any emotion.

Many people find that when they have done this exercise a few times, it becomes easier to understand other emotions with the Processing Emotions exercise. I am grateful to my friend Genpo Roshi for the inspiration for this exercise.

THE APEX OF COMPASSION

Read the whole exercise through before you start.

1. Let yourself focus on the feeling that is bothering you, whatever it is. It could be sadness, it could be fury, or it could be something as vague as a dull emotional ache.

2. As you notice it, ask if there is anything that
   feeling would wish to say to you. If there
   is, make a note of it; if there is not, that is
   absolutely fine.

3. Now notice the shape of where you feel that
   feeling and imagine giving it a color—so
   you are visualizing that feeling as a colored
   shape. Now move it out so that you imagine holding the feeling in your left hand, in
   front of you and a bit to the left.

4. Now I'd like you to think of the polar opposite of that feeling. For example, the opposite of sadness would be love, the opposite
   of fury would be peace, the opposite of a
   dull ache would be lightheartedness.

5. Bring that opposite feeling to mind and
   notice how it feels. Notice the shape of how
   you feel it and give that shape a color.

6. As you notice it, ask if there is anything that
   feeling would wish to say to you. If there
   is, make a note of it; if there is not, that is
   absolutely fine.

Continued

7. Now imagine placing that opposite positive feeling in your right hand, in front of you and slightly to your right.

8. Now move your attention up into your head and from that position experience the presence of both feelings—the original difficult one on your left and its polar opposite on your right.

9. Continue to feel the two emotions simultaneously for one minute, and as you do that your emotional system will recalibrate so that you can experience that difficult emotion at a safe level and stay in touch with its positive opposite.

10. Finally, from this position in your head ask if there is anything that either of those feelings would wish to say to you. If there is, make a note of it; if there is not, that is absolutely fine.

This exercise helps your feelings to recalibrate. Because you have now acknowledged them, your emotions no longer need to shout so loud, so they will not overwhelm you.

Mapping a Happy Future

You have released the emotions that were blocked, so you are free now to move forward with all your emotional awareness.

Now it is time to bring together all the work you have done with this system to integrate more and more happiness into your future. This exercise builds on the values you have realized in Chapter 6 and projects them into your future to focus your unconscious mind on bringing more and more fulfillment and happiness into your life.

First of all, we need to establish how your mind represents the future, then we will use that format to boost your future happiness with all the work you have done. All of this will be reinforced every time you listen to the hypnotic trance.

This system is far more powerful than just visualization on its own. Placing the images in a time context makes them more real and compelling, which alters your attitudes about yourself and your future at the conscious and unconscious levels.

My friend Dr. Richard Bandler has made a remarkable discovery about how we code time. The following steps will show you how your mind represents your future.

DISCOVER YOUR TIMELINE

Read the whole exercise through before you start.

1. Think of something you do each day, like brushing your teeth or eating lunch. When you picture yourself doing that tomorrow, is the image in front of you, up or down, to the right, or to the left? How far away is it? Point to it now.

2. Now think about doing the same thing next week. Is the picture more to the right or to the left? Higher or lower? Closer or further away? Once again, point to where you "see" the image in your mind.

3. Next think about doing the same activity one month into the future. Is the picture more to the right or the left? Higher or lower? Closer or further away?

4. Finally, imagine yourself doing that same activity in one year's time. Where is that picture—left or right? Higher or lower? Closer or further away?

5. Now review all those pictures and imagine they are all connected by a line—like doing a giant "connect the dots" drawing in your mind. This is your "timeline"—the way your unconscious mind represents time.

Now we are ready to install a new, compelling vision of your happy future. You are going to build a picture that represents the happiness towards which you are moving.

For example, when I did this with a client recently, he saw himself sitting by a lake watching his children playing in the water. He knew the place that he was imagining but what was hugely different for him was that in this picture he could see he was totally relaxed and in the moment. He wasn't fretting about all the problems at his business, he wasn't fussing with the barbecue. He was really peaceful and enjoying the sunshine and seeing his children play.

SETTING UP A HAPPY FUTURE

Read the whole exercise through before you start.

1. Imagine a year has passed and the level of happiness in your life has rocketed.

2. Design a scene of all the wonderful things that have happened to make your life brilliantly happy. See all the big changes and also notice small details, like how you are sitting or standing and the expression on your face. Find all the signs that you are truly contented. Make sure you can see yourself in that picture looking truly happy.

3. Now take that picture and place it exactly where you visualized one year ahead on your timeline. Make the picture big, bright, and colorful. You will know you are doing it right because it feels really good just to imagine it.

4. Next, you are going to fill in the steps between one year ahead and the present moment.

Make a slightly smaller picture of what will need to happen on the way to that super level of happiness and place it a few months before the big picture of a year ahead.

Make an even smaller picture of what will need to happen before that, and place it a few months before the second picture.

Continued

Make an even smaller picture of what will happen as you increase your happiness before that and place it a few months before the third picture.

You should now have a succession of pictures connecting the present with your compelling happy future. The images should get progressively bigger with better and better things happening in them.

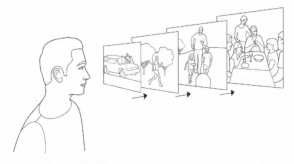

5. Look at those pictures and let your unconscious mind lock in the road map to your happiness over the next year.

6. Now, float up and out of your body and into each picture. Take a few moments to fully experience each step you will be taking on the path to deeper and richer happiness.

7. When you get to the big picture of your ideal scene, really allow yourself to enjoy experiencing it fully.

8. Finally, come back to the present and look out once again at your future timeline. You can feel confident that you have now created a map for your unconscious to guide and assist you as you build up your happiness throughout the next year and beyond.

Tuning In to Our Deepest Bliss

I want to tell you now about a discovery that has been hailed by scientists, philosophers, religious leaders, and scholars as the most important breakthrough in meditation in the last 2,000 years.

Most meditations involve relaxation and the repetition of a word or mantra over and over again to create a still mind and a profound feeling of calm and peacefulness. With years of practice, meditators can build on this stillness to achieve the highest state of awareness. In Buddhism, it is called "Samadhi." In Zen it is "Satori." The Hindus call it "the bliss of all bliss." In Christianity, it is sometimes referred to as "Christ Consciousness." Throughout history, people have committed their entire lives in the hope of receiving just one taste of this state of enlightenment.

Recently, my friend Genpo Roshi, a Zen master from an ancient lineage, has made an astonishing discovery that means that the holy grail of spirituality—a glimpse of enlightenment—is now available to everyone.

Zen is not a religion. It is a practice or discipline, like yoga, juggling, or even driving a car. In traditional Zen practice, monks meditate for many years to reach Satori. Genpo Roshi has combined elements of Zen meditation and Western psychology to create a procedure that allows human beings to make a jump to the core experiences of meditation, which have been the goal of the Zen tradition for centuries.

Research at the University of Utah shows that people without any prior experience of meditation, from any background, can use this procedure to achieve in minutes the same states of consciousness as monks who have meditated for years.

In the hypnotic trance, I am going to introduce you to the experience that Genpo Roshi has made available to us. Within the frame of the trance this experience will be as gentle or as deep as is right for you at the time you are listening.

Genpo calls his procedure Big Mind. When you do Big Mind, you connect to the infinite consciousness that is your birthright. It feels like bliss, an overwhelming feeling of happiness, peace, and tranquility.

Where does this feeling come from? Well, maybe it has been there all the time. Think of it like this: A baby has no idea that it's separate from anything. It certainly doesn't know that it is separate from its mother. It can't tell the difference between itself and anything else. It perceives itself as part of the ocean of infinity.

As a baby grows up into a child, it begins to discover that it is separate from the rest of the world. It learns how to manipulate and control things, and how to criticize and evaluate and protect and desire. These abilities help it navigate its way through the world, but they also result in a mind constantly filled with thoughts about getting and protecting. This constant noise in our heads is the only true obstacle to experiencing the infinite pure consciousness that we experienced as a baby.

How It Works

It's common to hear people refer to a part of themselves. For example, we might say a part of me wants to go the cinema, but a part of me wants to stay at home. This is simply a way of describing aspects of our psyche.

The process of the Big Mind meditation involves establishing communication with those parts of ourselves that seek to control, evaluate, protect, and desire. Big Mind invites them to reposition themselves for a short while so they are no longer in the forefront of our awareness. Gradually we stop overevaluating and controlling. You let go of your everyday awareness, your mind becomes quiet, and your consciousness expands so you become one with everything.

Another way of thinking about it is this. Everything in the universe is made of the same thing, atoms and molecules vibrating in different forms. In fact, if we leave earth and travel out into the galaxy we can see planets orbiting around a central orb or sun. If we travel back to earth and take a microscopic voyage inside a drop of water, we can see a living universe that is made of atoms and molecules, like planets orbiting around a sun. Every atom is a microcosm of the universe. The Samadhi or Satori state of enlightenment involves an expansion of consciousness where people report feeling like a wave in an infinite ocean of the energy of the universe, at one with and part of everything.

Underneath all the doing and judging and thinking that we do in our everyday life, this blissful state—Nirvana, Samadhi, Satori—is always present. When we move beyond our everyday thinking, this simple state of being is right here, right now, waiting for us to awaken.

Big Mind doesn't require any previous experience. You don't have to know about meditation, and you don't have to be religious. You don't even have to believe anything. You can be as skeptical as you want and it still works. Just listen to the hypnotic trance.

Backbone of Happiness

This system helps you build the framework that is the backbone of happiness. For each person the details and events that make you happy will be different. Your happiness is unique.

I strongly recommend that you keep practicing all the techniques you need even if you begin to feel happier straight away. All of them will enhance the happiness you already feel. Sooner or later, life will bring more challenges your way, and that is when you will be grateful for your practice. You will know how to find moments of joy and feel the deep background of happiness, even when times are hard. You will find more enjoyment and happiness in times and places you really didn't expect to.

Being Happy

Being happy is simple. Being unhappy is complicated. Happiness teaches us that deep down we are all already connected to each other, and it reminds us to enjoy that.

Happiness reminds us that every day is precious. Not one day of our life will be repeated. Each day we can choose happiness, we can choose to live by our values, and we can choose to be grateful for the amazing possibilities we are given.

Over 50 scientific tests have shown that when large groups of people are peaceful and happy there is a measurable reduction in violent crime. Every day you are happy increases the sum total of happiness in the world. When enough of us live happily by our values we actually make a real contribution to everyone's happiness. So don't keep your happiness to yourself. Spread it around and it will make you happier still.

There is an old Chinese proverb that I'd like to leave with you:

If you want happiness for an hour—take a nap.

If you want happiness for a day—go fishing.

If you want happiness for a year—inherit a fortune.

If you want happiness for a lifetime—help someone else.

14-DAY

Gratitude Journal

DAY 1

Today, I am grateful for . . .

1...
....

2...
....

3...
....

4...
....

5...
....

6...
....

DAY 2

Today, I am grateful for . . .

1 ....

....

2 ....

....

3 ....

....

4 ....

....

5 ....

....

6 ....

....

DAY 3

Today, I am grateful for . . .

1..

....

2..

....

3..

....

4..

....

5..

....

6..

....

DAY 4

Today, I am grateful for . . .

1 ....

....

2 ....

....

3 ....

....

4 ....

....

5 ....

....

6 ....

....

DAY 5

Today, I am grateful for . . .

1 ....

....

2 ....

....

3 ....

....

4 ....

....

5 ....

....

6 ....

....

DAY 6

Today, I am grateful for . . .

1 ....

....

2 ....

....

3 ....

....

4 ....

....

5 ....

....

6 ....

....

DAY 7

Today, I am grateful for . . .

1...

....

2...

....

3...

....

4...

....

5...

....

6...

....

DAY 8

Today, I am grateful for . . .

1 ....

....

2 ....

....

3 ....

....

4 ....

....

5 ....

....

6 ....

....

DAY 9

Today, I am grateful for . . .

1..

....

2..

....

3..

....

4..

....

5..

....

6..

....

DAY 10

Today, I am grateful for . . .

1 ....

....

2 ....

....

3 ....

....

4 ....

....

5 ....

....

6 ....

....

DAY 11

Today, I am grateful for . . .

1..

....

2..

....

3..

....

4..

....

5..

....

6..

....

DAY 12

Today, I am grateful for . . .

1..

....

2..

....

3..

....

4..

....

5..

....

6..

....

DAY 13

Today, I am grateful for . . .

1..

....

2..

....

3..

....

4..

....

5..

....

6..

....

DAY 14

Today, I am grateful for . . .

1..

....

2..

....

3..

....

4..

....

5..

....

6..

....

INDEX OF TECHNIQUES

ACKNOWLEDGMENTS

My thanks to Dr. Richard Bandler, Dr. Ronald Ruden, Dr. Robert Holden, Michael Neill, Doug Young, Genpo Roshi, Kevin Laye, Steve Witchett, Jonn Serrie, Kate Davey, and Mari Roberts.

HYPNOTIC TRANCE MUSIC BY JONN SERRIE
"Stratos" from *And The Stars Go With You*
www.thousandstar.com

We hope you enjoyed this Hay House book. If you'd like to receive our online catalog featuring additional information on Hay House books and products, or if you'd like to find out more about the Hay Foundation, please contact:

Hay House, Inc., P.O. Box 5100, Carlsbad, CA 92018-5100
(760) 431-7695 or (800) 654-5126
(760) 431-6948 (fax) or (800) 650-5115 (fax)
www.hayhouse.com® • www.hayfoundation.org

• •

Published and distributed in Australia by:
Hay House Australia Pty. Ltd., 18/36 Ralph St., Alexandria NSW 2015
Phone: 612-9669-4299 • *Fax:* 612-9669-4144 • www.hayhouse.com.au

Published and distributed in the United Kingdom by:
Hay House UK, Ltd., Astley House, 33 Notting Hill Gate,
London W11 3JQ • *Phone:* 44-20-3675-2450 • *Fax:* 44-20-3675-2451
www.hayhouse.co.uk

Published and distributed in the Republic of South Africa by:
Hay House SA (Pty), Ltd., P.O. Box 990, Witkoppen 2068
info@hayhouse.co.za • www.hayhouse.co.za

Published in India by: Hay House Publishers India, Muskaan Complex,
Plot No. 3, B-2, Vasant Kunj, New Delhi 110 070 • *Phone:*
91-11-4176-1620 • *Fax:* 91-11-4176-1630 • www.hayhouse.co.in

Distributed in Canada by:
Raincoast Books, 2440 Viking Way, Richmond, B.C. V6V 1N2
Phone: 1-800-663-5714 • *Fax:* 1-800-565-3770 • www.raincoast.com

• •

Take Your Soul on a Vacation

Visit www.HealYourLife.com® to regroup, recharge, and reconnect with your own magnificence. Featuring blogs, mind-body-spirit news, and life-changing wisdom from Louise Hay and friends.

Visit www.HealYourLife.com today!

Paul McKenna, Ph.D., is described by Ryan Seacrest as "a cross between the Dr. Phil and Tony Robbins of Britain." Recently named by the *London Times* as one of the world's leading and most important modern gurus, alongside Nelson Mandela and the Dalai Lama, he is Britain's best-selling nonfiction author, selling 8,000 books a week in 35 countries—a total of 8 million books in the last decade. He has worked his unique brand of personal transformation with Hollywood movie stars, Olympic gold medalists, rock stars, leading business achievers, and royalty. Over the past 20 years, Paul McKenna has helped millions of people successfully quit smoking, lose weight, overcome insomnia, eliminate stress, and increase self-confidence. Dr. McKenna has appeared on *The Dr. Oz Show, Good Morning America, The Ellen DeGeneres Show, Rachael Ray, Anderson Live,* and *The Early Show.* He is regularly watched on TV by hundreds of millions of people in 42 countries around the world.

Dr. McKenna has consistently astounded his audiences and clients by proving how small changes in people's lives can yield huge results, whether it's curing someone of a lifelong phobia or clearing up deepseated issues in a matter of minutes. He currently hosts his own TV show on Hulu, where he interviews the most interesting people in the world. His guests include Simon Cowell, Harvey Weinstein, Rachael Ray, Sir Roger Moore, Roger Daltrey, Tony Robbins, Paul Oakenfold, and Sir Ken Robinson. Website: www.mckenna.com

**FOR MORE INFORMATION
GO TO
mckenna.com**